Better nutri

by Gilly

Becoming a Better You

Better Meals.
Better Choices.
Better YOU.

First published by Fuzzy Flamingo 2021
www.fuzzyflamingo.co.uk

Paperback ISBN: 978-1-7399631-2-5

Welcome

Now let's get started!

Hello and welcome to *Better Nutrition by Gilly* – you've made the first step to an improved version of you!

Let's lay a few things down ...

I am NOT going to give you a set of rules to follow. Nope!
I won't even recommend a 'diet'. I'll simply teach you how to make better choices and to change your thought process regarding food and exercise.

I want you to live better and feel better! The educational layout of the programme helps teach you about health, better body composition (less fat and more muscle tone) and a healthy and happy mind.

This programme will help with:

- Improving weight and appearance
- Improving sleep
- Reducing stress levels
- Increasing energy levels
- Being in a better mood and feeling more in control of your emotions
- Reducing the risk of today's killers (e.g. diabetes, coronary heart disease and hypertension)

This booklet will show you just a few tips and tricks to help you get started and put you in the right direction.

Remember: **WE DO NOT DIET**. I provide **LONG-TERM, SUSTAINABLE** and **SENSIBLE** weight loss.

There are NO restrictions, weighing in or measuring, just learning and finding the path towards the better you!

Let's make it happen!

Contents

Before You Start

Know Your Portions

Most people think controlling portions means counting calories. But I think that there is a better, much easier way – the hand measurement system. Your hand is proportionate to your body, its size never changing, and it's handy because it's always with you, thus making it the perfect tool for measuring food and nutrients – minimal counting required.

Palm — 1 Protein

Fist — 1 Vegetable

Thumb — 1 Fat

Cupped Hand — 1 Carb

The Plate Portions

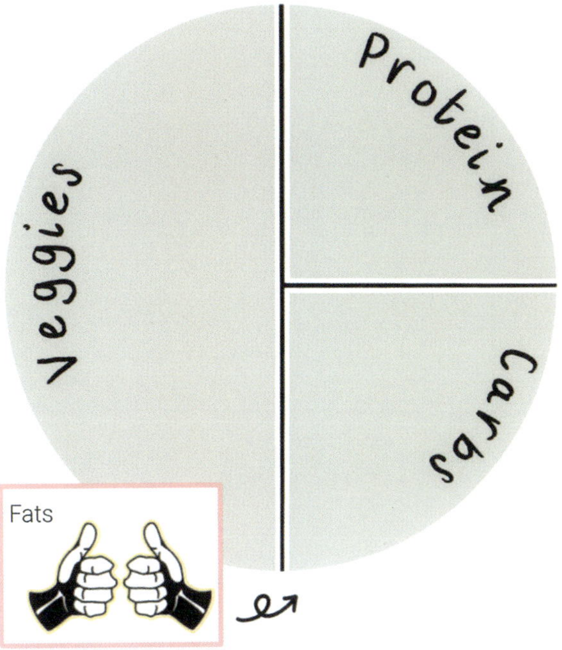

Portion Sizes: Male V Female

**for all portion sizes specific to your goals please check with Gilly

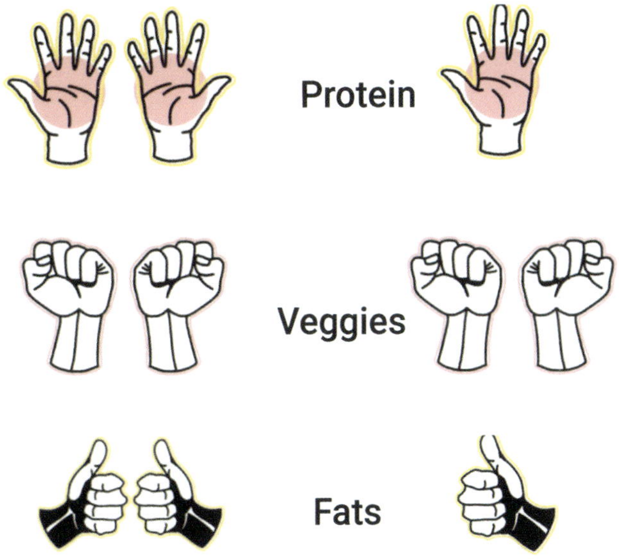

2-3 thumbs of healthy fats for men and 1-2 thumbs for women

Getting Prepared

Get Organised

Look ahead and start planning each week / day; look for busy days and schedule exercise, shopping and food prep around them. A good routine will help on the road to success.

It's also wise to start a meal plan; writing down what you will eat in a week and only buy the ingredients you need. This makes for less waste, less temptation and a clearer mind.

Sleep More, Stress Less

Sleep is also incredibly important as this is when your body does most of its hard work (digesting and taking all of the nutrients from the food and water you have had during the day and converting it into energy for the next day ahead).

Be Accountable

We're only human, and it's key to remember this! With this programme there are NO restrictions, so it is important that you stay mindful of what you eat, and if you have something that isn't necessarily on plan, be accountable for your actions; it's not good, it's not bad, it's HUMAN.

Set Goals

Keeping goals for yourself is a great way to keep on the path towards a better you.

It's also important to keep small when goal setting; trying to think of the now and the build up to success rather than the very end.

So, it's good to set SMALL, ACHIEVABLE goals regularly, as this will also help your mind see improvements as you're on your journey to a better you.

Water Is Your Best Friend

8 glasses a day should suffice; the work our bodies do can be very exhausting and dehydrating so it's very important to keep drinking water to help our body keep up the good work!

Get Ahead

On this programme it's great to get ahead and plan meals for the future, so it's good to explore new recipes to try. On the Better app I use with clients I share additional recipes and videos etc. If you are interested in knowing more then please book a free discovery call HERE>>>https://p.bttr.to/312Scn1

There are also plenty of good recipes online (just be sure to check the ingredients!).

At Better Nutrition by Gilly I don't whip you into submission by making huge statements about how incredibly strict and restrictive I want you to be. I aim to teach you how to make small changes which are sustainable and easy! Before you know it these changes become habit (just like brushing your teeth).

Let us educate you step by step

1. Eat Slowly

"Eat slowly!? Are you people crazy??? Who has the time for that during a busy work day? Grab a burger and GO!"

Eating slowly and taking the time to enjoy your meal, preferably sitting down, will help your body digest the food and help it catch up with your mind in regards to how much you're eating.

2. Little Changes

"Fine, fine! I'll get a side salad with that burger and maybe just a few potato chips, while I work on that report. Oh yeah, and throw in a Diet Coke instead of a regular!"

Just like small goal setting, it is better to add changes in small increments to help the journey seem easier and to also implement habit building.

3. Homemade

"Hey, I can make my own burger ... and it's pretty good! I whipped up the burgers on my food prep day so I had them handy. I got some nice tomatoes, salad and wholegrain buns from the local market, pretty darn tasty!"

Food prep days and making your own food is great as it's a great way to save time and makes the busy day lunch break easier to manage. But you also know what is going into your food, so you can remain mindful of what you eat and be in control of your gut.

4. Sensible Choices

"Let's do the burger without the bun ... And I'm going to sit, take my time and enjoy this. I need a quiet break from the day. Hmm, what to drink? Water's good!"

As time goes on, these habits will get stronger and making sensible choices will become easier and, almost, like second nature. Trust the process and before you know it you will be on the steady path to a better you!

Why wait – well, actually – you're not waiting; you're already doing it! But now you have the knowledge, don't wait until tomorrow...

Let's get started now! Right in THIS moment!

Don't make a HUGE statement about changing X,Y,Z, how you're going to do A,B,C – just make a start and go from there! No pressure, no gigantic expectations, just the satisfaction you've made the start!

How long before you want to see results? JUST DO IT! Don't put it off; "I'm too busy right now, I have this event, that lunch, that wedding, a night out, parties to attend..." Recognise all of these ...

Change your life TODAY

Who do you want to be? Take a moment to indulge me here at Better Nutrition by Gilly. Find a quiet corner, close your eyes and take a few VERY deep breaths. Now, think about a time in your life when you felt INCREDIBLE. This can be you at a wonderful weight, fabulous fitness level or just full of crazy confidence. Now freeze-frame YOU feeling like that. Your hand is on the remote control, finger in 'pause' and you are watching yourself at your VERY BEST. What do you see? Facial expressions, energy, body language ... break it all down. What were you wearing, who were you with, what can you see, smell, hear and do you see yourself looking, feeling and being great?

Memorise this moment in time and save it for later. It will be extremely useful in future behavioural change work! Whilst you're on this programme we promise to guide you and help you find your feet as you walk the path to this better you. So, if you're ready, take a deep breath and ...

Let's do this thing!

Tracking

It's very important to keep track of your meals (including your drinks), sleep, mood and number of fruits and vegetables you have per day.

On page 9 you will find a tracker that you can choose to print and complete if it helps you, as being accountable and having regular, individual feedback is very helpful to clients.

Page 8 is an example of a completed tracker to give you an idea of what information to include.

You can choose to write on, draw on, or colour in your tracker. Whatever works best for you.

DAY	MON	**TUE**	WED	THU	FRI	SAT	SUN					DATE	1st September
WEEK	1	2	**3**	4	5	6	7	8	9	10	11	12	

MOOD

STRESS

SLEEP	0 - 1	1 - 2	2 - 3	3 - 4	4 - 5	5 - 6	**6 - 7**	8 +		
F & V	1	2	3	4	5	6	**7**	8	9	10

BREAKFAST

Protein: one palm eggs (2 in total). Carbs: one slice wholegrain, seeded rye toast. Healthy Fats: 1/3 avocado mashed. Veggies/salad: half a plate of mushrooms, tomatoes and spinach

LUNCH

Large warm, chicken salad with Protein (one palm chicken), Carbs (one cupped hand new potatoes with skin). Fats (drizzle of olive oil). Veg/ Salad - half a dinner place of lettuce, tomatoes, peppers, mini-corns and cucumber.

DINNER

Veggie Stew with one palm mixed beans (not in sauce) in a homemade tomato based sauce with garlic. Lots of chopped veggies (carrots, celery, peppers, swede) and one cupped hand of brown basmati rice (cooked weight is the cupped hand measure). H-Fats: two thumbs of almonds after the meal

SNACKS

celery and peanut butter (two thumbs for the PB)

DRINKS

Water, Water, Juice, Water, Water, Water, Tea

How much walking did you do today?	8,560 steps	What time did you wake up?	6.45 am
How much exercise did you get today?	45 minutes	What time WILL you go to bed?	10pm

DAY	MON	TUE	WED	THU	FRI	SAT	SUN		**DATE**			
WEEK	1	2	3	4	5	6	7	8	9	10	11	12

MOOD										
STRESS										
SLEEP	0 - 1	1 - 2	2 - 3	3 - 4	4 - 5	5 - 6	6 - 7	8 +		
F & V	1	2	3	4	5	6	7	8	9	10

BREAKFAST

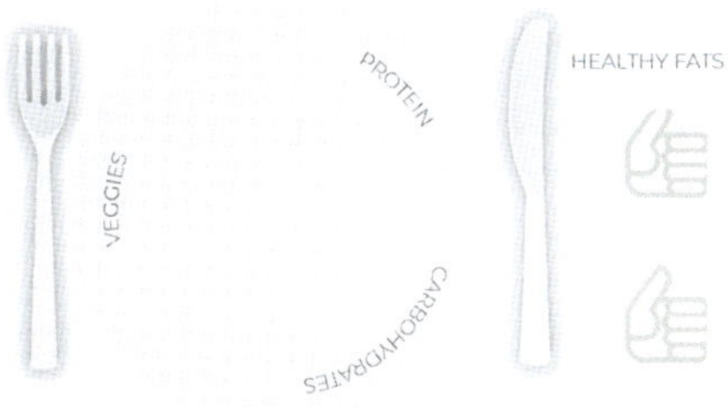

LUNCH

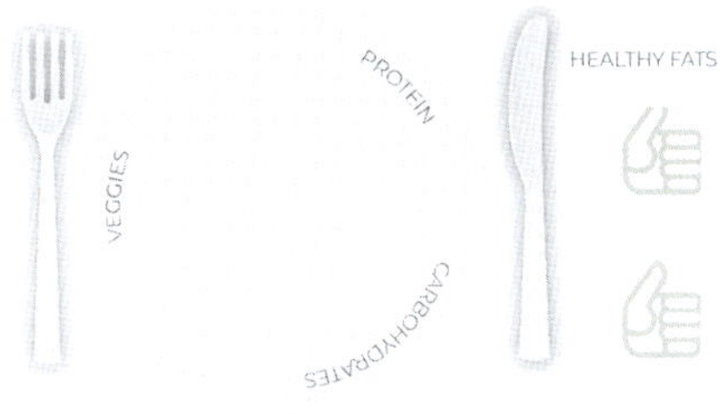

DINNER

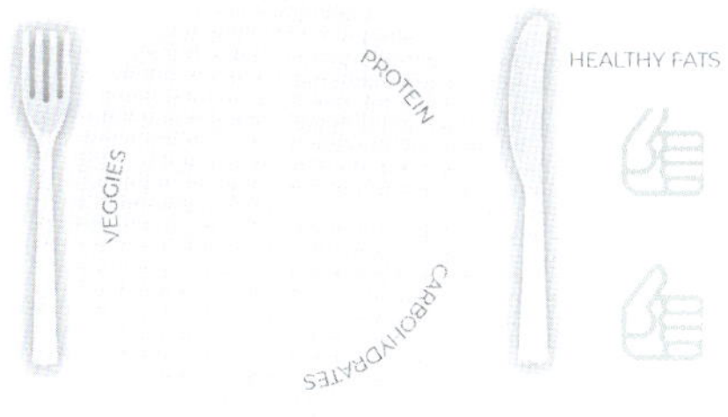

SNACKS

DRINKS

How much walking did you do today?	Minutes and/ or steps	**What time did you wake up?**	
How much exercise did you get today?	Minutes and/ or steps	**What time WILL you go to bed?**	

1

WELCOME TO

WEEK ONE

Getting Started

Welcome to your marathon (this isn't a sprint). There is no need to know everything from Day 1. This is an educational, more sustainable lifestyle programme offering support and balance.

Please get in touch if you are concerned about anything but following the steps below should help:

1. Check the Meal Plan (for reference and ideas only) and also the blank template which you can print out and complete if that helps.
2. Decide to follow the 'Meal Plate' or 'Hand Guide' for portions.
3. Start to complete your tracker using portions.
4. Any questions please email me on gilly@betternutritionbygilly.com
5. Consider your goals. You may already have something in mind. Ask yourself 'why is 'X' important to me' and then again 'and why is that'. Often what we think we want isn't the driving factor but more of that will follow.

Getting Active!

You may not have a dog but the chances are you know people who do! Many schedule their dogs for two walks per day and won't deviate from this, no matter the weather or their mood.

Why are we any different?

Create a schedule for your activity. Doing this on a Sunday for the week ahead creates 'intention' and you can start visualising attending those sessions (or doing that activity) and thinking about the value that it brings.

You can discuss (or negotiate in some cases) with your significant others and make sure you factor in all other commitments.

Have you thought about when is best for you (e.g.: before or after work), how long you have and what you like doing? It doesn't have to be a big gym session or a triathlon, as something like a brisk walk or gardening is classed as activity. The government guidelines are here: https://assets.publishing.service.gov.uk/government/uploads/system/uploads/attachment_data/file/829884/3-physical-activity-for-adults-and-older-adults.pdf

What will I do to be more active?

	M	T	W	T	F	S	S
Frequency							
Intensity							
Type							
Time							

Getting Shoppy!

I have been revisiting all of my resources produced over the last 4 years and ensuring that the material is up-to-date and in line with my beliefs about nutrition **ALWAYS** based on scientific facts. I am not a chef and so amazing recipes are not created by me but I will be sharing the recipes I love and that fit with your programme. I will **ALWAYS** credit the companies who have put these together. The recipes in this book are from That Clean Life: https://thatcleanlife.com/about

For now, think **REAL**. How would our grandparents and their parents have eaten? They would be shocked at the amount of plastic we get through and most would have shopped at the butchers, greengrocers, fishmongers or grown their own produce. Some may even have had chickens and fresh eggs daily. The milkman delivered in glass bottles which were recyclable.

If you want to really dig deeper and know more about how our food industry went crazy then see here (https://michaelpollan.com/books/in-defense-of-food/) for Michael Pollan's *In Defence of Food* and you'll learn about nutritional claims companies make, why diets don't work and where we went wrong!

For now, please don't overthink things. This programme is working specifically on what you need whilst, at the same time, offering some education on science, debunking myths and, **MORE IMPORTANTLY**, helping you to recognise your healthy and unhealthy habits and keep you accountable rather than making you count points, consider 'sins' or good and bad foods (food doesn't have emotions, so isn't naughty)!

I have edited the guide below to help you with the type of foods that will take you towards health and away from disease.

SUGGESTED SHOPPING (COMPLETELY OPTIONAL)

No	Animal Proteins	Fish & Seafood	Veg Proteins	Protein Portions	Veggies	Veggie Portions	Fats	Fat Portions
1	chicken	white fish	beans	WL female = one palm (100g) any protein for breakfast, lunch & dinner	green	Go wild. Eat as much as you can here. I suggest a minimum of two fists but also consider half of your plate with greens & colours (eat a rainbow)!	extra virgin olive oil	All – 1 – 2 thumbs per portion of breakfast, lunch & dinner plus one thumb before bed with protein
2	turkey	salmon	lentils		green		avocado	
3	lean beef	king prawns	split peas	WL male = 1.5 to 2 palms (150g-200g) any protein for breakfast, lunch & dinner	red		nut butters	
4	lamb	sardines	chickpeas		purple		walnuts	
5	goat	tuna	quinoa	Maintenance female = 1.5 palms (150g). Maintenance male = 2-2.5 palms (200g-250g) any protein for breakfast, lunch & dinner	pink		almonds	
6	lean chicken / turkey / lamb / beef mince	mackerel	eggs		berries (blueberries, raspberries, greenberries, redberries, strawberries)	Fruits are slightly different, more to follow!	coconut oil	

CARBS ARE NOT THE ENEMY!

I am going to be talking carbs shortly but aim for wholegrains. These are way better for healthy, slower digestion. These will be a quarter of your plate or 1-2 cupped hands (depending on the individual). Here are some examples:

Again, I am not a chef and each person will be adding / removing foods from their meals, so 'one size won't fit all'. I am happy to share the recipes I think are useful and tasty.

Getting Visual!

This picture is of me in my happy place (just south of Valencia), at the beach, close to my previous 'home'. I went there many mornings, early, to walk my little rescue-Princess, Poala (we call her P for short) and to have my quiet time before my crazy-life started. I believe in the power of meditation but also believe that the method is down to you and your preferences. Even now, I seek out nature and take the dogs early, without my phone (well how did you take this photo you might ask... hmmmmmmm)?!? I avoid people and have some 'me' time.

Can you start thinking about your 'happy place'. Think selfishly.

ABSOLUTELY NOTHING WRONG WITH THAT.

Feel free to describe that in your journal somewhere or use the space below. There is no obligation. You might just want to visualise your happy place and that's fine. This is your journey and there are no rules.

Print and stick your own photo here!

Use this space to describe your happy place

Getting Measured!

One of the main questions I am asked is "when will you do my measurements"?

My response is two-fold 1) which ones and 2) why?

Princess Poala is modelling a scale, a tape measure and some skin-fold calipers. These all measure but how accurate are they? Lots of things can mean our measures are not consistent (e.g.: practitioners' inexperience, faulty equipment, different methods of measuring, environment and even time of day / month). I am not categorically saying 'don't' use them but understand their limitations and ask if these numbers will help your health, and in particular your psychology. If not, then why bother?

Body Mass Index (BMI) and Hip to Waist Ratio are both pretty ancient and 'ballpark' measures used but neither tell us the whole story. For example; a gymnast or athletic 'type' might measure poorly on the hip to waist ratio (thinking of straight up and down types who might still have a good body composition).

An International rugby player might be 'Obese' on the BMI scale but have very good body composition (as the scale doesn't account for body fat, muscle, water, bone, connective tissue, etc.).

Then digging deeper we don't know the type of fat that a person has and whilst my skin-fold calipers (below) can 'estimate' how much subcutaneous (under the skin) fat is on an area of the body, the technique requires a high level of skill to get accurate results (some would say 10,000 clients' worth of practice).

Some gyms now have body composition scales and people seem to enjoy knowing their numbers here. These scales use bio-electrical impedance (a small electrical current runs up through your leg and across your pelvis then back down your other leg) and estimates the amount of resistance from body fat. Simplified, greater body resistance means a higher fat percentage as fat contains less water than muscle, so it's more dense than muscle and more difficult for a current to travel through. It's guesswork (and 15-40% inaccurate). It doesn't account for gender, age, ethnicity, activity levels or where you store fat (visceral fat around the abdomen increases your risk of diseases such as diabetes, heart disease and Alzheimer's).

Generally, most people are already aware of whether they are in good shape or not. This doesn't mean supermodel or athlete material but just a good weight for their health. This might not be within the BMI or waist to hip circumference 'ranges' (as in my shared guide) and these are only designed to be guide measures.

The String Test

Watch this video from the BBC (https://www.bbc.co.uk/programmes/p062c0tf) that demonstrates how to perform the string test. A test that measures your waist to height ratio.

So what do I prefer clients to use (more useful than numbers)?

Height to waist ratio. This will give you an indication of visceral fat, which is the kind we would ideally reduce for health reasons.

Your clothes. If your favourite jeans start loosening off and are more comfortable then you know you're improving (although you may need new jeans, so please don't invoice me)!

How you feel. Improved mood with less 'swings', happier, more confident, etc.

Your movement. I've had clients who struggled to tie their shoelaces but after some weight management commitment they feel elated that the task feels easy!

Your strength and recovery. If you work out then maybe you feel stronger, can manage more and need less rest and recovery.

Your sleep. By improving quantity and quality you may also reduce your visceral fat (more to follow).

Your stress levels. Anxiety, feeling out of control, etc., can also improve with nutrition and lifestyle improvements.

Consistency. Less hunger and cravings and more energy (no explanation needed here). Your daily HEC (hunger, energy and cravings) check gives me a lot to go on.

The DEXA Scan. If you're still adamant that using numbers is the best measure then please feel free to use the gold-star of measures (at between £150 – £200 per appointment).

What will you use to measure success?

DAY SIX

Did You Know?

Did you know that the food we eat combines with tiny chemical reactions within our cells? These interactions are directly responsible for our health.

We are what we eat!

DAY SEVEN

Day Off!

Tasks to complete:

RECAP

From this week what resonates with you the most? I suggest making a note about your favourite modules, videos and recipes so that you can easily come back to them.

Use this space to make a note about your favourite modules, videos and recipes

Weekly Reflection:

Think about what you have learnt this week and what resonates with you the most.

Book a FREE call with Gilly!

Enhance your progress with a FREE 15 minute consultation,

simply see here to book:

https://p.bttr.to/2OI0AIn

Join the community on social media:

@BetterNutritionby Gilly Facebook and Instagram

2

WELCOME TO

WEEK TWO

What are Macronutrients?

Macro is the shortened term for macronutrients. I think of them as the 'main' food groups and they have the following calorific values:

- **Protein (PRO)**: 4kcal per gram (meat, fish, seafood, eggs, quinoa, beans)
- **Carbohydrates (CHO)**: 4kcal per gram (sugars, starches and fibre found in fruits, grains, vegetables and milk)
- **Fats (FAT)**: 9kcal per gram (healthy fats come from plants including avocados, nuts, chia seeds, and olive oil). Eggs are classed as dietary cholesterol but contain many micro nutrients (B2 selenium, vitamin D, B6, B12 and zinc, iron and copper). Eggs also contain a substantial amount of protein. There are a few other types of fat but we will cover these later.
- **Alcohol**: 7kcal per gram

The amount your body needs can be calculated by working out lots of different, puzzling, equations. Total Daily Energy Expenditure (TDEE) is calculated by adding together a whole load of lengthy science-stuff:

BMR (Basal Metabolic Rate) + TEF (Thermic Effect of Food) + NEAT (Non Exercise Activity Thermogenesis) + Thermic Effect of Activity (TEA)

Breaking it down, Total Daily Energy Expenditure (TDEE) means the calories we use just by being alive, digesting food, day-to-day activities and exercising. Then (and here's where it gets tricky), depending on your lifestyle and set goals, your TDEE is divided between the three macronutrients (PRO, CHO, FAT) to form something we call the 'macronutrient split'.

Don't get too concerned about this. Research shows us that this can be miscalculated and, rather than advising people on what exact percentage split they need, the general population (including me) need to concentrate on 'balanced meals', three times per day consistently.

You might hear people say things like "I'm cutting" (reducing) or "I need to shred" (lose) fat or "She's looking ripped" (lean). In my experience, this type of 'diet' and restriction leads to 'bouncing out', regaining weight and feelings of failure. It simply isn't sustainable. My role is to remove stress, concerns about calculations and obsessions with numbers, as I want my clients to succeed and enjoy food in a simple way whilst learning the necessities.

Let's look at calories per gram. Protein (PRO) and Carbohydrates (CHO) offer 4kcal / gram, FAT provides 9kcal / gram and alcohol is 7kcal / gram. Whilst there are more calories, per gram, in fats, they are essential to give your body energy, to support cell growth, to protect your organs, to keep your body warm, to allow for the absorption of nutrients (vitamins A, D and E wouldn't be absorbed without fat) and to produce important hormones too. It's about choosing the right type in the right amount.

Warning:

I have heard people say "It fits my macros" as they devour a pizza, chips and chocolate cake. You shouldn't be eating **ANY** foods to fulfil the percentage macros advised. The loss in valuable nutrients can be dangerous for your health. On paper you could be meeting your maconutrient needs, but in reality you could be feeding your body with yukky, processed foods. You have to consider all of the micronutrients as well as the macros. These are your vitamins and minerals and play a VITAL role in fulfilling your optimum health. More to follow on those little blighters.

Another thing to consider are physique characteristics and these may be linked to metabolic differences in people. This means that we would need to catagorise a person in terms of their body type and adjust the macronutrients to maximise their chance of success in reaching their goals. This isn't as simple as looking at a person and guessing.

Exercise:

Macros are dependent on an activity, an exercise level or a sporting event. Your days might be very different in terms of your activity. Let's presume that a macro-split would be:

35%PRO, 40%CHO, 25%FAT (equal to 700kcal PRO, 800kcal CHO and 500kcal FAT)

If I decided to run a 15km race and my necessary calorie intake was guestimated at 2,000kcal then the day before the race my macros could change to:

20%PRO, 70%CHO and 10%FAT, as I would need the extra CHO for energy in the race (equal to 400kcal PRO, 1400kcal CHO and 200kcal FAT)

The reality is that my calories are estimated here and I am not an elite athlete who needs to worry about this. I need consistency with my three meals per day with my goals to maintain a healthy weight. I want to avoid illness and disease in the future. I also want to fit into my jeans without a fight.

Finally:

Sorry to break this to you, but 100g of chicken does not equate to 100g of PRO and nor does the weight to CHO grams work out exactly. On average 100g chicken breast provides 31g (or under) of PRO, 0g CHO and 3.6g FAT. This is why we ask you to use visuals and your own calculation tools (your hands or the plate guide)!

The palm, fist and thumb are a good indication of portion control and do not require getting into a tizzy over the numbers. (See page 3 for a reminder!)

Tasks to complete:

Your Macronutrients

Are you using your hands or the plate guide? Consider some of the feedback you've had regarding your meal choices. What is your main area of improvement so far?

Use this space to think about your macronutrients.

Tofu & Broccoli Salad with Peanut Sauce

4 servings

50 minutes

Ingredients

1 1/16 lbs Tofu (extra-firm, pressed, cubed)
2 tbsps Tamari (divided)
2 tbsps Rice Vinegar (divided)
1 1/2 tbsps Sesame Oil (divided)
1 tbsp Arrowroot Powder
1/4 cup All Natural Peanut Butter
2 tbsps Water
3 cups Broccoli (chopped into tiny florets)
1/3 cup Radishes (thinly sliced)
1/4 cup Raw Peanuts (roughly chopped)

Directions

1. Preheat the oven to 400°F (204°C) and line a baking sheet with parchment paper.
2. Add the tofu to a large baking dish along with half of each the tamari, the rice vinegar, and the sesame oil. Marinate for 15 minutes. Add the arrowroot powder and gently toss to combine.
3. Add the tofu to the baking sheet, spacing the pieces out. Bake for 25 to 30 minutes, flipping halfway through.
4. Meanwhile, add the peanut butter and water to a bowl along with the remaining tamari, rice vinegar, and sesame oil. Mix well until combined.
5. Add the broccoli and radishes to a salad bowl and add the peanut dressing and toss to combine. Top with crispy tofu and peanuts. Enjoy!

Notes

Leftovers: Refrigerate in an airtight container for up to three days.
Serving Size: One serving is about 1 1/2 cups of salad.
Nut-Free: Use sunflower seed butter and omit the peanuts.
More Flavor: Add chili flakes, sriracha, and/or grated ginger to the peanut sauce. Garnish with cilantro.
No Arrowroot Powder: Use cornstarch instead.

What, Why, When?

Creating Good Habits – Start With PRECISE Goals

Welcome and congratulations. You've made the decision to change.

My point? You have already made the commitment. Now we work on the finer details to ensure success early and build on that. My job is to make you feel comfortable and able.

This task is a very important starting point. Imagine telling someone how to travel from London to Liverpool with an instruction "It's up North" and not helping with the exact location on a map, travel considerations (mode of transport, travel time, timetables, etc.) and what might be helpful to take on the journey. Vague isn't going to get anyone anywhere.

Please take time to consider this task and preferably find a quiet corner away from kids, partners, work and pets! Just you.

Before we start, you need a pencil and a piece of paper (apologies to anyone under 25 years old who may be wondering what I am referring to. Just take out your smart phone and ask Siri to record your answers)!

Most people believe that exercise followed by nutritional changes will get them into their best shape BUT they ignore the 'why', 'when' and 'how'. Unfortunately, without understanding 'how' you can't really stick to anything. You need to plan and ask yourself a question.

What is important to me?

Just take a second and think about this. Telling yourself "to lose weight" or "get healthy / fit" is not enough. Write down the main problem, which has prompted you to start this program. It can be a reason or a feeling.

1) So why are you here / on this programme?

WRITE THIS REASON / FEELING DOWN

Use this space to record your reasons or feelings for joining this programme.

There is a good chance that this isn't the first time you have tried something lifestyle based (positively or negatively) and have experienced success vs failure. There are goals we know and there are new goals. It's important that when you reach goals that you celebrate and then set new ones. We are ever evolving.

2) Let's visualise YOU at your INCREDIBLE BEST:

Visualisation isn't mumbo-jumbo. It's what all professional athletes practise and in competitive situations it is the difference between first place and 'who remembers where you came'.

Tasks to complete:

Find a quiet moment, close your eyes, take 10 very deep breaths (I prefer breathing in for 4, hold for 7 and breath out very slowly for 8, but choose a pattern that is comfortable for you and repeat around 4 times). Then think:

What type of person will I be in 6 months' time?

Imagine you are watching this NEW 'Future YOU' in a movie. You can see who you will be.

WRITE THIS DOWN, including where you are, what you are wearing, who is with you, how you feel and what you see and smell... every little element. Do not skip details.

Use this space to visualise YOU at your INCREDIBLE BEST.

3) Break down your goals from vague to precise:

Underneath your 'Future You' movie script write another list:

1. 6 weeks
2. This week
3. Today

Next to each time frame add where / what / who you WILL be.

Examples:

- **6 weeks**: I will lose 6kg / I will rejoin the rugby team / I will fit into my jeans / I will be stronger / I will be more educated about nutrition / I will feel more 'in control'.
- **This week**: I will lose 1kg / I will complete my activity sessions on 'X days' / I will cement my goals / I will plan my meals / I will read each 'module' at 'X' time every day.
- **Today**: I will complete this task / I will list my meals for today / I will declutter my kitchen (removing foods which will take me and my family away from health) / I will walk 'X' number of steps.

"I will... ": The goals must specifically state what is going to happen. They must be clear and easy to understand and should not be ambiguous. For example, rather than you stating that you would like to 'get fit' you can create a more specific goal such as "I will run a 5K in 2 months time in my local town." This can be health, weight, image, event or feelings related.

"When": Please set a date (e.g.: stipulate the date at the end of your programme time). Your date might be longer as this is your time frame, but better to understand and state that date now. You could write this on a calendar, in a diary or set electronically through your phone, etc. Know this date.

Use this space to break down your goals from vague to precise.

4) How confident are you with your goals?

Another question I will ask you is "How confident are you"? Give this a rating of 1 to 10 (10 being like a superhero)!

MOOD									
1	2	3	4	5	6	7	8	9	10

We will talk about anything you rate under a 9 or a 10. It could mean that your goal is too big or you just need some help being specific.

Eating For Change

This is a great short video designed to make you think about your own relationship with food and the habits we have formed over decades (including 'diet culture'): https://www.youtube.com/watch?v=fbeFn1Xcqo4

Tasks to complete:

Eating for Change

Most nutrition studies looking at longevity and quality of life are looking at populations who eat 'real' food. Not only that but it is about those communities enjoying and respecting food. It's about your attitude to food (and eating) as an individual, within a couple or as a family.

Consider your attitude to food, how you eat and how you feel about eating 'real' foods. This task doesn't require anything from you but to provoke thought and a discussion around what and how you eat.

After watching the video you can use this space to consider your attitude to food, how you eat and how you feel about eating 'real' foods.

Chili Lime Tempeh Bowls

4 servings
1 hour 40 minutes

Ingredients

1/2 tsp Smoked Paprika
2 tsps Chili Powder (divided)
2 tsps Cumin (divided)
1 tsp Garlic Powder (divided)
3/4 tsp Sea Salt (divided)
3 Lime (juiced)
1/4 cup Vegetable Broth
1 tsp Maple Syrup
9 ozs Tempeh (cut into thin pieces)
1 Red Bell Pepper (thinly sliced)
1 Green Bell Pepper (thinly sliced)
1/2 Yellow Onion (thinly sliced)
1 tbsp Water
1 cup Quinoa
1 Avocado (sliced)

Directions

1. In a shallow bowl or zipper-lock bag combine the paprika, half of the chili powder, half of the cumin, half of the garlic powder, and two-thirds of the salt. Stir in the lime juice, vegetable broth and maple syrup and mix well. Add in the tempeh and gently toss to coat the tempeh in the marinade. Let the tempeh marinate for at least one hour or up to 8 hours. If marinating for longer than 1 hour keep the tempeh in the fridge.
2. When the tempeh has finished marinating, preheat your oven to 375°F (190°C) and line a large baking sheet with parchment paper.
3. Add the peppers and onion to a large mixing bowl. Add the remaining chili powder, cumin, garlic, salt and water and toss to coat the vegetables. Transfer the seasoned vegetables to the prepared baking sheet and arrange on one-third of the pan.
4. Gently toss to coat the tempeh in the marinade again then arrange the tempeh evenly on the remaining two-thirds of the baking sheet. Ensure the pieces are not overlapping or touching. Discard any remaining marinade. Bake for 28 to 30 minutes, flipping halfway through, or until the vegetables are tender.
5. Meanwhile, cook the quinoa according to the package directions.
6. Divide the quinoa, tempeh and vegetables between bowls and serve with the sliced avocado. Enjoy!

Notes

Leftovers: Refrigerate in an airtight container for up to two days.
More Flavor: Add cayenne pepper for a spicy tempeh. Use oil to roast the vegetables.
Additional Toppings: Cilantro, salsa, yogurt, diced tomatoes or sliced green onions.

DAY THIRTEEN

Did You Know?

Did you know that we have a massive 25 foot canal inside our bodies? This digestive canal breaks down our food so we get the nutrients we need to stay healthy.

DAY FOURTEEN

Day Off!

Book a FREE call with Gilly!

Enhance your progress with a FREE 15 minute consultation, simply see here to book:
https://p.bttr.to/2Ol0AIn

Join the community on social media:
@BetterNutritionby Gilly Facebook and Instagram

Weekly Reflection:

Think about what you have learnt this week and what resonates with you the most.

3

WELCOME TO

WEEK THREE

Focus on Diabetes Mellitus

The Basics – Type 1 and Type 2 Diabetes Mellitus

In 2012, The American Diabetes Association reported that almost 30 million Americans suffered from diabetes. The UK's National Health Service (NHS) state that 3.9 million people are living with diabetes equating to one in 16 people. In the UK alone, this figure has more than doubled since 1996.

By 2025, it is estimated that five million people will have diabetes in the UK (NHS, 2015).

In the USA, 1 in 3 people will have T2 diabetes by 2050 (Centre for Disease Control and Prevention, 2010).

Given the increasing prevalence of diabetes I feel you should be VERY aware of the facts. Keep reading! Type 2 Diabetes is a disease you can avoid (and can be placed into remission).

First – let's look at insulin. You've heard about it but do you really understand what is happening?

Insulin is a hormone made by the pancreas. It allows the body to use sugar (glucose) from carbohydrates in the food that you eat (for energy now or in the future).

Insulin is like a strict yoga teacher! It keeps your blood sugar level from getting too high (hyperglycemia) or too low (hypoglycemia). It creates balance.

T1 Diabetes Mellitus (T1DM):

It is usually diagnosed in children and young adults (also known as juvenile diabetes), although adult onset T1DM cases have increased over the last 10 years. Only 5% of people with diabetes have this form of the disease. However, with the help of insulin therapy and other treatments, even children can manage their condition and live long, healthy lives.

The upside: Exercise is good for everyone and especially important for adults and children with diabetes. Exercise can help control blood glucose plus there are all of the other benefits (heart, muscles, mood, weight, confidence, etc.).

The downside: Blood glucose (blood sugar) levels can drop during or after exercise so sufferers need to check their levels often.

Blood glucose levels during / after exercise: If it's low then eat a snack and wait until blood glucose comes up but even if your blood glucose isn't low you may still need to eat a snack. This depends on the type of activity and how the body reacts to the activity.

T2 Diabetes Mellitus (T2DM):

Type 2 diabetes is the most common form of diabetes and may, in small cases, be genetic BUT mainly is caused by lifestyle factors and our choices. This includes our nutritional choices, stress management techniques, sleep protocols and activity choices. In a nutshell, the body causes blood glucose levels to rise higher than normal (called hyperglycemia) and the body doesn't use insulin properly (insulin resistance). At first, your pancreas makes extra insulin to try and compensate but then it can't make enough insulin to keep blood glucose at normal levels.

Facts:

- Diabetes causes more deaths a year than breast cancer and AIDS combined.
- Having diabetes nearly doubles your chance of having a heart attack.
- T1DM is mainly caused by genetics and unknown factors.
- T2DM is mainly caused by lifestyle factors.
- Being overweight may increase your risk of developing T2DM
- A diet high in calories from any source contributes to weight gain.

Drinks (not just food):

Research has shown that sugary drinks are strongly linked to T2 diabetes. These will raise blood glucose and can provide several hundred calories in just one serving!

These are the culprits:

- regular fizzy drinks
- fruit punch
- fruit drinks
- energy drinks
- sports drinks
- sweet tea / sweet coffee

Just one standard fizzy drink can = approximately 150 calories and 40 grams of carbohydrate. This is the same amount of carbohydrate in 10 teaspoons of sugar!

Tasks to complete:

Consider your Carbs!

What carbohydrate foods and drinks do you consume? Make 2 lists:

Make a list of those which are healthy (higher fibre and natural) vs those which are not taking you towards health (processed foods, sugary drinks, coffee shop specials, processed snacks, white / beige fast release carbs, etc.).

Are you surprised about your consumption or is there something you could avoid?

Consider the connection between your carb choices and where this places you on the 'Health Scale'. Can you make some choices which move you up the scale towards better health (and reduce your risk of disease)?

Use this space to list the carbohydrate foods and drinks you consume.

Veggie Scramble with Strawberries

1 serving

15 minutes

Ingredients

4 Egg

1/8 tsp Sea Salt (divided)

1 tsp Extra Virgin Olive Oil

1 Red Bell Pepper (finely chopped)

1 Tomato (medium, diced)

1 stalk Green Onion (chopped)

1 cup Strawberries (chopped)

Directions

1. Whisk the eggs in a bowl and season with half of the salt. Set aside.

2. Heat the oil in a pan over medium heat. Cook the peppers for about five minutes or until tender and just browned. Add the tomato and green onion and cook for two to three minutes more until the tomatoes have softened. Season the vegetables with the remaining salt.

3. Push the vegetable mixture to one side of the pan and pour the eggs into the empty side. Stir the eggs frequently as they cook and incorporate the vegetables into the egg once the eggs are cooked through. Serve with strawberries and enjoy!

Notes

Leftovers: Best enjoyed immediately.

More Flavor: Add dried herbs and spices like garlic powder or parsley.

No Red Pepper: Use any colour of bell pepper.

Like it Spicy: Add red pepper flakes or jalapeno pepper.

No Strawberries: Serve with a different fruit instead.

Dietary Fats

Dietary Fats – the Good, the Bad and the Ugly!

There are 5 categories of fats which we will look at (from very unhealthy to healthy) as follows:

- **TRANS**
- **SATURATED**
- **DIETARY CHOLESTEROL**
- **POLYUNSATURATED**
- **MONOUNSATURATED**

> **"A small amount of fat is an essential part of a healthy, balanced diet. Fat is a source of essential fatty acids, which the body cannot make itself. Fat helps the body absorb vitamin A, vitamin D and vitamin E. These vitamins are fat-soluble, which means they can only be absorbed with the help of fats."**
>
> **(NHS, 2019)**

The fats we consume are essential for so much more, including insulation (our warmth), to build cell membranes (the vital exterior part of each cell) and the sheaves surrounding our nerves, hormone production, immune and brain function. Some fats may even decrease the risk of cardiovascular disease and are essential for blood clotting, muscle movement and inflammation. Fats, as we know from the NHS, are essential for the absorption of certain vitamins, improve satiety (keep us fuller for longer) and improve the flavour of foods we consume. Wow, who knew?

Even though fats have so many benefits, we have to consider the 'type' of fat we are consuming. Harvard Medical School have quite a nice summary:

> **"Avoid the trans-fats, limit the saturated fats and replace with essential unsaturated fats."**

TRANS-FATS:

These are found in solid margarine and commercially made pastries, cakes, sweets, fast foods and breads.

It is a byproduct of a process called hydrogenation that is used to turn healthy oils into solids and to prevent them from becoming rancid (spoiled). Trans-fats have no known health benefits and there is no safe level of consumption.

Eating foods rich in trans-fats increases the amount of harmful LDL (loser) cholesterol in the bloodstream and reduces the amount of beneficial HDL (happy) cholesterol. Trans-fats create inflammation (linked to heart disease, stroke, diabetes and other killer diseases). They contribute to insulin resistance (where your insulin has stopped working as effectively to deal with glucose), which increases the risk of T2 diabetes mellitus. Even small amounts of trans-fats can harm health.

Harvard Medical Centre report that just 2% of calories from trans-fat consumed every day would increase the risk of heart disease by 23%.

SATURATED:

This type is solid at room temperature and found in some cheaper red meats, whole milk / dairy foods, coconut oil (although this we will discuss later) and many processed baked goods and fast foods.

A diet high in saturated fats may increase total cholesterol (although there is debate about this). This then may encourage blockages to form in the arteries of the heart and elsewhere in the body. I recommend that my clients restrict their saturated (animal source) fats to under 10% of their daily food intake per day (this is why I ask you to use thumbs to measure).

DIETARY CHOLESTEROL:

Found in animal products (eggs, liver, kidney, shellfish). 20% of the cholesterol in your bloodstream comes from the food you eat. Your body makes the rest.

Dietary Cholesterol performs 5 main functions: helps create the outer coating of our cells, makes the bile acids required for digesting food in the gut, allows the body to make Vitamin D, needed for the production of hormones and essential for brain function.

Some studies have shown that dietary cholesterol does not increase blood cholesterol but rather the transporters (carrying cholesterol) are problematic, not the cholesterol we eat.

Now the Healthy Ones: Monounsaturated and Polyunsaturated Fats

Healthy fats (from vegetables, nuts, seeds and fish) are liquid at room temperature, not solid. The two categories are monounsaturated and polyunsaturated fats.

POLYUNSATURATED FATS:

Some sources are corn oil, sunflower oil and safflower oil. These fats are essential fats, meaning that they're required for normal body functions but your body can't make them (so you need to consume them). Polyunsaturated fats are necessary to build cell membranes and the covering of nerves, blood clotting, muscle movement and inflammation.

Our two main types of polyunsaturated fats are omega-3 fatty acids (O3) and omega-6 fatty acids (O6). The numbers refer to the distance between the beginning of their carbon chain and the first double bond (refer to this video: https://www.youtube.com/watch?v=srfkLNH_QdQ but don't worry too much about the structure side of things). Both types offer health benefits.

Eating polyunsaturated fats in place of saturated fats or highly refined carbohydrates reduces harmful LDL (loser) cholesterol and improves our cholesterol profile. It also lowers triglycerides (blood fats).

Good sources of O3s are the SMASH oily fish (salmon, mackerel, anchovies, sardines and herring), flaxseeds, walnuts, canola oil and non-hydrogenated soybean oil.

O3s may help prevent and even treat heart disease and stroke.

All the benefits: O3s may reduce blood pressure, raise the HDL (happy) cholesterol, lower triglycerides, help prevent lethal heart rhythms from occurring and may help reduce the need for cortico-steroid medications in people with rheumatoid arthritis. Studies have also linked O3s to other health improvements, which include the reduced risk of dementia (although this is a controversial area of study with no conclusive evidence).

O6s are linked to protection against heart disease but it is worth noting that our consumption of O6s, in the UK, outweighs the consumption of O3s by around 14:1, which is a problem. Basically we should aim for way more O3s and less O6s TO If you would like to know more then book a free Discovery Call.

The UK daily guideline for TOTAL fat is 70g per day and no more than 20g for women and 30g for men should be as saturated fat per day. However, this is only a guideline and depends on an individual and their goals (weight management can be maintaining, increasing or decreasing body weight) and how nutritious the fat is that we choose (healthy vs unhealthy).

MONOUNSATURATED FATS:

All monounsaturated fats are liquid at room temperature and types are olive oil, peanut oil, canola oil, avocado, most nuts as well as high-oleic (meaning high in monounsaturated fats) safflower and sunflower oils.

One of the biggest studies of nutrition was the Seven Countries Study (1960s), which revealed that people in Greece and the Mediterranean enjoyed a low rate of heart disease even though they consumed a relatively high-fat diet. The main fat in their diet wasn't saturated (animal) fat but was olive oil, which contains mainly monounsaturated fat. The more Western diet was much higher in saturated and lower in monounsaturated fats and those populations studied had a much higher rate of heart disease.

After all of that, which fats are you going to start increasing and which will you reduce?

Tasks to complete:

Consider your dietary fat choices!

That was quite a lot to take in today. Can you identify the foods you currently consume which are TRANS, SATURATED, DIETARY CHOLESTEROL, POLY & MONOUNSATURATED fats?

Is there anything you need to change? Are you always sticking to the thumb(s) for your portion control?

Use this space to look at the foods you currently consume and see if there is anything you need to change.

Habits and Goals

I thought this piece would resonate with some of you. We are usually conditioned to 'diet' for a set amount of time but with no real plan of what happens after 'D Day'.

One of the main problems I see with new clients (particularly around 'New Year's resolution' time in January or when they are planning for a big event like a holiday or a wedding) is that they try and implement too much at once and in too short a time. Pressure!

In my experience, around 8% of people setting NY resolutions actually make it past day 8.

Training hard 6 days a week and eating only limited calories will most likely result in a big crash and burn.

Psychologically, this is not sustainable and physiologically this is exhausting.

The second thing I see is no clear action plan with achievable short-term goals. Visualisation of where you WILL be in the end is VERY powerful. There is an NLP (Neuro Linguistic Programming) technique I like to call 'your movie' where I ask clients to visualise watching themselves in a movie theatre. They are the star in their own movie and they are sitting, with the popcorn, watching themselves at the event (let's say wedding). It's an amazing production with no expense spared and they see every detail. We put the movie on slow motion and I ask the client to explain every fine detail. You worked on something similar earlier this week.

Visualisation is just one technique and is very important for setting shorter-term goals. If someone is looking to change 5 dress sizes in one year then this needs to be planned in small doses. This week and this month is as far as I like to go. When I speak to you in your video 'Weekly Catch Ups' you will note we talk about your goals, weekly. Not something 12 months away or a huge weight loss goal.

Thirdly, if someone isn't going to address other potential barriers (sleep, stress, other commitments and prioritising) then an 'all-out' programme isn't going to last for long.

I like to start slowly with clients and, in fact, some complain that 'this isn't what they are used to' or 'isn't quick enough' (I make it very clear with clients that I don't work on the 'quick fix').

Habits:

Together we set an achievable new habit which they stick to for 1-2 weeks. This breeds success. Success is contagious. We then set another habit which the client adheres to for 1-2 weeks, and another and another. This is progressive learning in the same way we don't jump into the jump and perform a 120kg back squat for reps! This would take weeks, months or years for some people adding a couple of tiny semi-kilos at a time. We are building (think Lego)!

Willpower can run out and the idea is to find some strategies in advance that clients can use to build on other successes they've had in their life. That's why I build on habits (as above).

The same applies to our metabolism when being too restrictive. As the caloric intake decreases, the body adapts by lowering resting metabolism. In order to prevent fat loss (and keep us alive), the body becomes more efficient in utilising the reduction of calories. We need healthy food and to be consistent with three meals per day.

As above, it's the same with exercise. When you do a certain activity over and over, muscles remember the activity and start doing them more efficiently (so you can build the weight and maintain integrity with the movement). If you don't train then you don't improve strength. If you eat too few calories, your metabolism adapts by slowing down.

The moral of the story: 'slowly, slowly catchy monkey'!

This isn't to say that clients don't start feeling much better after 10 days to 2 weeks on a sensible nutrition programme. Detoxification, feelings of control (in terms of an improved relationship with food) and success through incremental habit building are noticeable very early on.

Please, trust the process and don't sweat the small stuff. Let me look after your food and allow yourself to be accountable to me via your daily Food / Mood Journals, daily (evening) HEC checks and by keeping in touch via the message and video-chat systems. I am here to support (and nudge) you.

This is a journey and we don't want it to be abruptly ended if you become fed up, restricted or bored!

Tasks to complete:

Revisit your goals!

Please reread your initial goals (in your weekly report or something you have confirmed with / to yourself). You should be clear and happy about your goals.

Use this space to look at your goals and make any tweaks.

Citrus Coconut White Fish

2 servings
20 minutes

Ingredients

1 tbsp Extra Virgin Olive Oil
1/2 Yellow Onion (medium, chopped)
2 Garlic (cloves, minced)
1 tsp Cumin
1/8 tsp Sea Salt
1/2 Tomato (large, diced)
1/4 cup Orange Juice (freshly squeezed)
1/4 cup Canned Coconut Milk (full-fat)
1/4 cup Cilantro (chopped)
2 Cod Fillet

Directions

1. In a pot just large enough to fit the fillets, heat the oil over medium heat. Add the onions and cook for three to five minutes or until the onions start to soften. Add the garlic, cumin, salt, and tomato and stir to combine. Cook for another minute.
2. Add the orange juice and simmer for two to three minutes until the tomatoes begin to soften. Stir in the coconut milk and cilantro and bring the liquid to a simmer.
3. Add the cod fillets to the pot and cover with the lid. Steam the cod for six to 10 minutes or until cooked through and flakey. The cooking time will depend on the thickness of the fillets.
4. Divide the filets between plates and top with the citrus coconut sauce. Enjoy!

Notes

Leftovers: Refrigerate in an airtight container for up to three days.
Fillet Size: One cod fillet is equal to 231 grams or 8 ounces.
Additional Toppings: More cilantro, lime wedges, or red pepper flakes.
No Cod: Use another white fish, like haddock, instead.
No Extra Virgin Olive Oil: Use avocado oil or coconut oil instead.

DAY TWENTY

Did You Know?

Did you know that we start to reduce muscle mass as we get older?

This can be 5lbs per decade and so we must make sure that we include the correct exercises to counteract this.

DAY TWENTY ONE

Day Off!

Book a FREE call with Gilly!

Enhance your progress with a FREE 15 minute consultation, simply see here to book:
https://p.bttr.to/2Ol0AIn

Join the community on social media:
@BetterNutritionby Gilly Facebook and Instagram

Weekly Reflection:

Think about what you have learnt this week and what resonates with you the most.

4

WELCOME TO

WEEK FOUR

22

DAY TWENTY TWO

What's The Best Diet?

Video – Dr. Mike Evans – What's The Best Diet?

This is a great video that explores some of the issues we have with nutrition (internal and external). Please take time to watch this.

Watch here:
https://www.youtube.com/watch?v=fqhYBTg73fw

Chewy Almond & Prune Bites

6 servings
15 minutes

Ingredients

1 cup Pitted Prunes
1/4 cup Cocoa Powder
1/4 cup Almond Butter
1 tsp Cinnamon
3 tbsps Hemp Seeds

Directions

1. Add the prunes, cocoa powder, almond butter, and cinnamon to a food processor and blend until well mixed and sticky.
2. Form into even balls with your hands, roughly one-inch in diameter. Roll each ball in the hemp seeds until evenly coated. Store in the fridge or freezer until ready to enjoy.

Notes

Leftovers: Refrigerate in an airtight container for up to one week, or freeze if longer.
Serving Size: One serving equals approximately two balls.
Nut-Free: Use sunflower seed butter, pumpkin seed butter, or tahini instead of almond butter.
More Flavor: Vanilla extract and/or your sweetener of choice.

The Science of Soreness

We all know about muscle soreness. Some (strange) people enjoy it but flapping about like a beached seal and not being able to scratch your head isn't our idea of fun!

Why do we get sore? Is it dangerous? Should we stop exercising? How do we know when it is dangerous (physio time) or just plain muscle soreness?

Here we go. In short, here is the science:

Placing any stress on your muscles after a period of inactivity OR if you are activating the muscles very intensively will cause small microscopic tears, known as micro-trauma, in the muscles. The body immediately starts to repair these tears by filling the muscle with oxygen and nutrients, which causes muscle swelling. The swelling nudges the nerves and they scream 'PAIN'!

DOMS (Delayed Onset of Muscle Soreness):

Muscles can also tighten up some time after exercise. DOMS can be felt as pain and stiffness in the muscles for 24 to 72 hours post-exercise. DOMS is most intense following exercises that focus on eccentric contractions where a weight is lowered or slowed (downward phase of a bicep curl, or downhill running).

DOMS can be prevented by gradually increasing the intensity of a new exercise program. While the soreness will usually disappear within 72 hours of onset, increased blood flow to the sore area, either by moderate intensity exercise or massage, may help alleviate soreness. Stretching does not prevent soreness; however, it is still important to perform some static (holding) stretches after exercise to maintain or improve flexibility.

Approach to help DOMS:

Hydration, fuelling, appropriate exercise progression and stretching will help prevent DOMS and maintain range of motion, respectively.

Poor Posture:

During periods of prolonged inactivity, for example, long days and weeks working at a desk, some muscles can get tight as a result of their restricted movement. When you are seated at a desk, your hips are in a bent, or flexed, position. This puts the muscles on the front of the hip (hip-flexors) in a shortened position, and the muscles on the back of the hip (glutes) in a lengthened position. In addition, as you sit at a desk reaching forward to work on a computer, your chest muscles (pectorals) will be in a shortened position, while your upper back muscles (rhomboids) will be in a lengthened position.

Over time, this can result in muscle imbalances with the shortened muscles becoming 'tight' and the lengthened muscles becoming weak. If you look around you, you'll notice many people have developed poor posture with forward rounded shoulders and underdeveloped glutes.

Approach to Help Poor Posture:

1. It is important to maintain PROPER POSTURE, even while seated.
2. You should also specifically STRENGTHEN THE SMALL MUSCLES which have become lengthened and weak.
3. Lastly, you should make sure to STRETCH THE TIGHT MUSCLES, specifically the chest and hips.

MUSCLE CRAMPS:

Another time when muscles tighten up is during exercise, for example, a muscle cramp. Cramps are unpleasant, often painful sensations caused by a variety of factors that include muscle fatigue, low sodium, or low potassium. Muscle cramps can also happen even when you're not exercising.

When muscles contract, the muscle fibres shorten, increasing tension in the muscle. When the contraction is completed, the muscle fibres lengthen and decrease tension. During a muscle cramp, however, the muscle fibres remain shortened and are unable to lengthen due to fatigue or improper hydration and nutrition. Forcibly stretching the muscle when it is in such a tight, contracted form can tear the muscle fibres and lead to injury.

Approach to Help Muscle Cramps:

1. Allow the muscle spasm to relax and recover before attempting to stretch out the cramp.
2. In order to prevent these from occurring in the future, make sure to be PROPERLY HYDRATED and PROPERLY FED, and not overly fatigued when exercising.
3. If engaging in exercise bouts lasting longer than 60 minutes, consuming an electrolyte replenishing drink may help prevent muscle cramps.

Tasks to complete:

Consider your stretching!

How often do you stretch? Do you engage in any yoga, Pilates or functional stretching?

There are a great number of apps available to help with stretching, here are a couple of favourites!

Nike Training Club

Available on the Apple App Store –

https://apps.apple.com/gb/app/nike-training-club/id301521403

Available on the Google Play Store –

https://play.google.com/store/apps/details?id=com.nike.ntc&hl=en_GB&gl=US

ROMWOD

Available on the Apple App Store –

https://apps.apple.com/us/app/romwod/id1175346453

Available on the Google Play Store –

https://play.google.com/store/apps/details?id=com.romwodllc.android&hl=en_GB&gl=US

Or try Mike Bines who offers an affordable monthly subscription for those interested in yoga and pilates plus other classes: https://www.facebook.com/mbpts/

Today is something to think about and nothing to complete.

Real Vs Processed Foods

There are two things to consider when looking at food choices. The first is quantity (we can measure in calories, portions and / or macronutrient percentages) and the second is quality, where we ask:

Is a calorie a calorie? Are 100 Kcals from a cheap fast-food burger and 100 Kcals from broccoli the same?

If you eat fewer calories than you use, will you lose weight?

The second point is down to the proven law of thermodynamics (if you want to know more please book a Discovery Call) but point #1 is flawed in a few ways.

With calories, we must consider the thermal effect of food. Calories are a measure of energy and our weight change depends on the balance between energy in versus energy out.

Energy out:

- physical activity (activity metabolism)
- energy to keep you alive at rest (basal metabolic rate)
- energy added to the body like amino acids to muscle and fat to fat tissues
- energy lost in waste (faeces and urine)
- energy used to digest the food you eat

Energy in seems simple: How many calories were in the spinach salad, turkey sandwich or ice cream that you ate? Wrong. Energy in is just as complex as energy out, because of the energy cost of digesting food.

Digesting food costs energy:

Have you ever wondered how celery has negative calories? It takes more energy to break down and absorb the celery than the celery contains. Eating costs calories such as chewing, swallowing, churning in the stomach, making the acid in the stomach, making the enzymes, to make the rhythmic muscular contractions (peristalsis) that drives food through, etc.

Within science we have three names for this:

- dietary-induced thermogenesis (DIT);
- thermal effect of food (TEF); or
- specific dynamic action (SDA).

On average, a person uses about 10% of their daily energy expenditure digesting and absorbing food, but this percentage changes depending on the type of food you eat. Protein takes the most energy to digest (20-30% of total calories in protein eaten go to digesting it). Next is carbohydrates (5-10%) and then fats (0-3%).

So, if you eat 100 calories from protein, your body uses 20-30 calories to digest and absorb the protein. You'd be left with a net 70-80 calories. Pure carbohydrate would leave you with a net 90-95 calories, and fat would give you a net 97-100 calories.

So the question is "Is a calorie just a calorie"? It seems that not only does macronutrient content change TEF, but processing also changes TEF.

Protein and fibre play the main parts here and, in essence, you could lose weight eating processed fast food BUT you can eat a lot more whole food (containing important nutrients and keeping you fuller for longer) and lose the same amount of weight.

If you didn't have enough reasons to avoid processed food when losing weight, add the reduced thermal effect of food to the list. Processed food takes less energy to digest and absorb compared to whole foods, so 100 calories of processed food ends up being more net calories than 100 calories of whole food.

If you're trying to lose weight, eat whole foods. If you're trying to gain weight you may find that you need to include a little more processed food for a while (although this approach requires caution).

So the BIG question is 'What is truly "whole" food'?

The majority of foods that we eat are in fact processed. Spinach that is cleaned and bagged-up, yoghurt made at home and even a boiled egg all qualify as processed foods because strictly speaking once a food is altered it is a processed food. But seriously, canning, cooking, freezing, dehydrating and milling might not be for foods full of artificial ingredients or nasties!

The United Nations have defined 4 categories as follows:

1. Unprocessed or minimally processed foods

If you consume an apple or eat a tomato from your garden you are eating an unprocessed food. As stated, most foods go through some sort of processing. Minimally processed foods such as chopped carrots (in packaging), chopped lettuce and raw nuts are healthy and the processing they have undergone are mostly for the sake of shopping. Minimally processed foods sometimes contain additives used to preserve the properties of the original food and to make transporting foods possible.

2. Processed culinary ingredients

Processed culinary ingredients are substances obtained directly from unprocessed or minimally processed foods or from nature. They are altered by processes such as pressing, refining, grinding and in other manners so that they can be used in the cooking process. Examples include sugar obtained from the cane, oats for your morning porridge, syrup from maple trees and vegetable oils extracted from olives or seeds.

3. Processed foods

Also known as 'Lightly Processed Foods', this category includes foods like tomatoes, green beans, tuna, and berries that are canned or frozen soon after harvesting. They may have one or two added ingredients (e.g.: salt, sugars or oils) and are usually no more than 3 or 4 ingredients. Commons foods such as breads, cheeses and pastas are examples of lightly processed foods. Packaged items with only a few high quality added ingredients (e.g. herbs, spices, oils) might also be considered lightly processed, such as some pasta sauces and salad dressings.

4. Heavily / ultra processed food

Many foods in this category are called "Junk Food". These are foods made with five or more ingredients and are filled with sugars, oils, fats, salt, antioxidants, stabilisers, and preservatives. Generally speaking, ultra processed foods include lots of added stuff that doesn't occur naturally. Nearly all the food in this category are unhealthy and eating too many foods in this category increases the risk of obesity and diabetes and they are associated with a heightened risk of cardiovascular disease.

When judging what's "whole" and "processed" foods, ask yourself:

- What's on the ingredient list?
- Do I recognise all these things?
- How many steps did this food take to get to me?
- Does this food come in a bag, box, or can?

For a real eye-opener (next time you're at the supermarket) take a look at the ingredients of a few different brands of yoghurt and compare them. Good quality plain yoghurt will have two ingredients: milk and bacteria. Other 'well-marketed' yoghurts will have things like sodium citrate, starches, gelatine, pectin, calcium phosphate, potassium phosphate and sodium phosphate. Do you know what these are?

You might also be surprised to see what is in cream. Plain cream is often milk with cheap emulsifiers and sweeteners such as dextrose.

Read labels and be aware of many ingredients, added sugars and additives and things you cannot pronounce!

Tasks to complete:

Check Your Processed Foods

What foods could you change so you are eating non-processed or minimally processed foods for the majority of the time?

Select three foods you currently consume and think about how they could be less processed.

Cucumber & Tomato Quinoa Bowl

2 servings
15 minutes

Ingredients

1/2 cup Quinoa (dry)
2 leaves Romaine (chopped)
1/2 Cucumber (medium, chopped)
1 Tomato (medium, chopped)
1 cup Chickpeas (cooked)
2 tbsps Feta Cheese (crumbled)
2 tbsps Lemon Juice
3 tbsps Parsley (chopped)

Directions

1. Cook the quinoa according to the directions on the package, and set aside.
2. Divide the chopped romaine equally between bowls or plates. Top with equal amounts of quinoa, cucumber, tomatoes, chickpeas, and feta.
3. Squeeze lemon juice overtop and garnish with parsley. Enjoy!

Notes

Leftovers: Refrigerate in an airtight container for up to four days.
Serving Size: One serving equals approximately two cups.
Make it Vegan: Use vegan cheese or omit the feta completely.
More Flavor: Cook the quinoa with broth instead of water. Add your favorite dressing overtop.
Additional Toppings: Olives, capers, avocado, or red onion.

DAY TWENTY SEVEN

Did You Know?

Did you know that we reduce our resting metabolic rate after 25 years old?

This means we start to slow down and it can be harder to lose weight. This can be altered through nutritional education and increased exercise.

DAY TWENTY EIGHT

Day Off!

Book a FREE call with Gilly!

Enhance your progress with a FREE Discovery Call:
https://p.bttr.to/312Scn1

Join the community on social media:
@BetterNutritionby Gilly Facebook and Instagram

Weekly Reflection:

Think about what you have learnt this week and what resonates with you the most.

5

WELCOME TO

WEEK FIVE

I am the TYPE of Person Who...

Firstly, when you think of people that you really admire (can be within your circles or famous types, etc.), what would you say about them (think why you admire them)?

Think morals, faith, fitness, kindness, work ethic... whatever you like. These things have drawn you to that person.

So if people were talking about you. What positive things would they say? What are your qualities?

"He / she is the type of person who / that..."

We aren't very good at identifying our own qualities and so asking a friend / loved one is a good idea. It certainly isn't being egotistical and PLEASE don't start justifying with 'but'. These are the things other people notice and like about you.

Next, start concreting positive traits and actions you have started picking up whilst on this programme and add "I am the type of person who / that... "

Examples:

I am the type of person who walks my dogs twice a day every day.

I am the type of person who enjoys shopping for, preparing and eating healthy food.

I am the type of person who drinks a glass of water first thing in the morning.

I am the type of person who loves training.

Now use this same positive affirmation for the traits / actions / practices that you WILL be starting to concrete (you might be practising these things at the moment). These will become ingrained in time with belief and consistency.

Examples:

I am the type of person who eats three balanced meals per day.

I am the type of person who eats real foods.

I am the type of person who piles half my plate with veggies / salad.

I am the type of person who drinks decaf.

You get my drift!

Tasks to complete:

Type of Person

Read through the notes on this module and start making a list. The more you keep telling yourself about who you ARE becoming, the more likely you are to start living those behaviours (and eventually they become ingrained).

What type of person are you? Make a list.

Use this space to go through the notes in this DAY and start making a list.

Orzo & Shrimp Pasta Salad

2 servings

15 minutes

Ingredients

1/2 cup Orzo (dry)
8 ozs Shrimp, Cooked (chopped)
1 head Endive (chopped)
2 cups Snap Peas (chopped)
1/2 cup Goat Cheese (crumbled)
1/4 cup Chives (chopped)
2 tbsps Lemon Juice
1/4 tsp Sea Salt

Directions

1. Cook the orzo according to the directions on the package. Once it's done cooking, set it aside and let it cool.
2. Add the orzo and the remaining ingredients to a large bowl. Toss until well combined. Divide onto plates and enjoy!

Notes

Leftovers: Refrigerate in an airtight container for up to four days.

Serving Size: One serving equals approximately 2 1/2 cups.

Gluten-Free: Use quinoa or brown rice pasta instead.

Dairy-Free: Use vegan cheese instead.

More Flavor: Add balsamic vinegar and your choice of additional spices and herbs.

Additional Toppings: Red pepper flakes, kimchi, sauerkraut, and/or your favorite dressing.

No Shrimp: Use chicken, turkey, edamame, marinated tofu, or chickpeas.

31

DAY THIRTY ONE

Healthy Habits in 30 Days

Matt Cutts – How to Change Your Habits in 30 Days

Every 30 days, Matt Cutts gives himself a new challenge: writing a novel, giving up sugar, even chewing more slowly. He says 30 days is enough time to develop a habit or just make life more interesting.

View here:
https://www.ted.com/talks/matt_cutts_try_something_new_for_30_days

Obesity & Coronavirus

Coronavirus is something that has affected all of us in one way or another. A study conducted by the US Centre for Disease suggests that obesity is the biggest risk factor for death from Covid-19 in under 50s.

Have a read through the below article from Oliver Morrison (Food Navigator) for more information.

Coronavirus and obesity: Doctors take aim at food industry over poor diets

22-Apr-2020 By Oliver Morrison

A cardiologist has blamed the food industry for 'normalising' ultra-processed junk food as more evidence emerges suggesting poor diet is the root cause behind increased mortality from Covid-19.

https://www.foodnavigator.com/article/2020/04/22/coronavirus-and-obesity-doctors-take-aim-at-food-industry-over-poor-diets

One Pan Lemon Spiced Chicken & Potatoes

4 servings
30 minutes

Ingredients

1 Lemon (divided)
1 lb Chicken Breast
5 cups Mini Potatoes (quartered)
2 cups Cherry Tomatoes (halved)
1 tbsp Extra Virgin Olive Oil
1 tsp Turmeric
1/2 tsp Ground Allspice
1/2 tsp Sea Salt
1/2 cup Plain Greek Yogurt
1/2 cup Parsley (chopped)

Directions

1. Preheat the oven to 400°F (205°C) and line a large baking sheet with parchment paper. Cut half the lemon into slices and set aside.
2. Add the chicken, potatoes, tomatoes, olive oil, turmeric, allspice, and sea salt to the baking sheet. Squeeze the juice from the remaining lemon over top and toss until well coated. Layer the lemon slices over top and cook for 25 to 30 minutes or until the chicken is cooked through.
3. Slice the chicken and garnish with yogurt and parsley. Enjoy!

Notes

Leftovers: Refrigerate in an airtight container for up to three days.
More Flavor: Add red pepper flakes, cayenne, paprika, black pepper, garlic and/or pomegranate seeds.

DAY THIRTY FOUR

Did You Know?

Did you know that protein is vital for every metabolic activity in our bodies? Protein contains the building blocks we need for growth, repair and energy conversion.

DAY THIRTY FIVE

Day Off!

Book a FREE Discovery Call:

https://p.bttr.to/312Scn1

Join the community on social media:

@BetterNutritionby Gilly Facebook and Instagram

Weekly Reflection:

Think about what you have learnt this week and what resonates with you the most.

6

WELCOME TO

WEEK SIX

Why Dietary Fibre?

Fibre is a plant-based carbohydrate. It is a term that, unlike other carbohydrates (such as sugars and starches like those in your vegetables), are not digested in the small intestine and make their way to the large intestine (your colon) without dilly-dallying!

Fibre helps to keep our digestive system healthy and can prevent constipation. Here's how: fibre bulks up stools, makes stools softer and easier to pass and makes waste move through the digestive tract more quickly.

The Benefits:

- Helps with weight management by keeping us fuller for longer. Fibre may also prevent the body from absorbing some of the calories in the foods you eat by binding with fat and sugar molecules as they travel through the digestive tract.
- Reduces the risk of Type 2 Diabetes by keeping blood sugar levels steady and helping to maintain a healthy weight.
- Lowers the odds of heart disease. For every 7 grams of fibre (eaten daily) the risk of heart disease drops by 9%. This is because fibre soaks up excess cholesterol in the system and transports it away, reducing clogging of the arteries.
- Increases healthy gut bacteria. Bacteria in the gut microbiome feed off fibre (and ferment in the gastrointestinal tract). They produce short-chain fatty acids that help lower systemic inflammation in the body, which has been linked to obesity and nearly every other major chronic disease. However, this requires some consistency with eating fibre daily. A fibre-rich diet can help increase these healthy bacteria in the gut and some may help to increase and produce substances that are thought to be protective (e.g.: short-chain fatty acids, a major source of energy for colon cells).

- Reduce the risk of some cancers. Every 10 grams of fibre you eat is associated with a 10% reduced risk of colorectal cancer and a 5% reduction of breast cancer risk. Also, the foods that contain fibre (e.g.: veggies and fruits) are also rich in antioxidants and phytochemicals that could further reduce the risk.
- Dietary fibre may help to protect against bowel cancer; although the reasons for this are not fully understood, the thinking is that fibre increases stool size, dilutes content and moves it faster through the gut so that waste products are not lingering. Some types of fibre may also help gut bacteria produce helpful chemicals (see below).

The World Cancer Research Fund (WCRF) estimate that 45% of bowel cancer could be prevented through diet, physical activity and maintaining a healthy weight.

- Beta Gluten (soluble) foods such as oats and barley contain a type of fibre known as beta glucan, which may help to reduce cholesterol levels if more than 3 grams are consumed daily, as part of a healthy diet.
- More 'regular' – Constipation is one of the most common gastrointestinal problems. Fibre increases the softness and bulky texture, which helps our waste pass through the system faster.
- A natural detox – Soluble fibre naturally cleans and promotes the elimination of toxins from your gastrointestinal tract by soaking up potentially harmful compounds (e.g.: estrogen and unhealthy fats) before they can be absorbed by the body. Also, insoluble fibre allows waste to move along more quickly which limits the amount of time that chemicals (e.g.: the chemical used to harden plastics – BPA, mercury and pesticides) stay in your system. The faster they go through you, the less chance they have to cause harm.
- Healthier bones – Some soluble fibres called 'prebiotics' (don't be confused with probiotics) are found in asparagus, leeks, soybeans, wheat and oats. They have been shown to increase mineral bioavailability. Calcium is one of the minerals and may help maintain bone density.

Soluble and insoluble fibre:

You may have heard of the terms 'soluble fibre' or 'insoluble fibre' and both describe the types of fibre in our diet. The science bods argue that these terms are no longer appropriate. They suggest that instead of soluble we use 'pectins and beta glucans' (e.g.: fruit and oats) and instead of insoluble we say 'including cellulose' (e.g.: wholegrains and nuts). Note that fibre-rich foods typically contain both types of fibre.

Fibre rich foods include:

- Wholegrain breakfast cereals, wholewheat pasta, wholegrain bread and oats, barley and rye.
- Fruit such as berries, pears, melon and oranges.
- Vegetables such as broccoli, carrots and sweetcorn.
- Peas, beans and pulses.
- Nuts and seeds.
- Potatoes with skin.

How much fibre do we need?

30g a day for adults (aged 17 yrs +). Unfortunately, we consume much less than this at around 18g per day.

To increase your fibre intake you could:

- Choose a wholegrain cereal like oats or a no added sugar muesli. Why not add some fresh fruit, dried fruit, seeds and / or nuts?
- Go for wholemeal or seeded wholegrain breads. White breads really have little nutritional value.
- Select wholegrains like wholewheat pasta, bulgur wheat or wholewheat basmati rice.
- Opt for potatoes with skins, e.g. baked potato, homemade wedges or boiled new potatoes.
- When snacking try a little fruit, vegetable sticks, rye crackers, oatcakes, unsalted nuts or seeds.
- Include half a plate of vegetables with meals. This can be a side dish / salad or added to sauces, stews or curries (also a sneaky way to get children to eat more veg).
- Keep a supply of frozen vegetables to add to meals.
- Add pulses like beans, lentils or chickpeas to stews, curries and salads.
- Have some fresh fruit (in moderation).

If you need to increase your fibre intake, it is a good idea do this gradually. It is also important to drink plenty of fluids (around 6-8 glasses per day for adults) and to try to be active, daily.

A healthy, balanced diet can provide enough fibre – especially if you eat your 5 A DAY and choose wholegrain foods and potatoes in skins. If you feel you are falling short then consider adding psyllium husk to your oats or in water (no strong taste) or even as a thickener in sauces.

Fibre and Irritable Bowel Syndrome (IBS):

Diet can play an important part in controlling IBS symptoms. If symptoms include constipation then gradually increasing dietary fibre intake may help (e.g.: wholegrains, oats, fruit, vegetables and linseeds may help to soften stools and make them easier to pass). However, if symptoms include diarrhoea it may be helpful to try reducing the intake of some high fibre food such as wholegrain breakfast cereals and breads.

NOTE – there is no 'one size fits all' diet for people with the condition. Keeping a food / mood journal helps with patterns and trying to ID food culprits. If you need further help, ask your doctor to refer you to a specialist.

Stay gut-happy!

Tasks to complete:

Consider your fibre intake

Are you including dietary fibre in all of your meals? Are you adding that half plate of salad / vegetables to all of your meals?

Where could you add fibre? Please feel free to message me if you would like help or (even better) suggest some additions to your meals and let me know!

Use this space to consider your fibre intake?

Chocolate Peanut Butter Banana Pops

10 servings

1 hour 30 minutes

Ingredients

2 Banana (large, ripe)
1/4 cup All Natural Peanut Butter
10 Popsicle Sticks
3 1/2 ozs Dark Chocolate (at least 70% cacao)
1 1/2 tsps Coconut Oil

Directions

1. Line a baking sheet with parchment paper.
2. Slice bananas into 1/2 inch thick rounds. Use a butter knife to spread peanut butter onto half of the banana slices. Place the remaining banana slices on top to create a sandwich. Transfer to the baking sheet.
3. Hold the sandwiches firmly on both sides with one hand and insert popsicle sticks through the middle of the top of each sandwich so they are sticking up vertically. Place in the freezer and let harden for ~30 minutes.
4. Fill one large pot with water and place a smaller pot inside. Bring to a boil then reduce to lowest heat. Ensure no water is able to escape into the smaller pot. Add the dark chocolate and coconut oil to the smaller pot and stir continuously until melted. Use a spatula to transfer all the chocolate into a small cup (note: this makes it easier for dipping).
5. Remove the bananas from the freezer and dip them one-by-one into the melted chocolate. Feel free to double dip if you have leftover chocolate. (If you are sprinkling with any toppings, do so quickly while the chocolate is still wet.)
6. Place the pops back onto the baking sheet with the popsicle sticks sticking up vertically. Place back in the freezer until chocolate is hardened (about 30 to 60 minutes). Enjoy right away or store in an airtight container for later.

Notes

No Peanut Butter: Use any type of nut butter, raw honey or Strawberry Chia Jam.

Optional Toppings: After dipping in dark chocolate, immediately sprinkle with toppings of choice like chopped nuts, shredded coconut or cacao nibs.

Bigger Pops: Slice the bananas into thicker rounds.

Creating New Healthy Habits

Most lifestyle changes (including our nutrition) rely heavily on understanding our own behaviours. You can have all of the knowledge in the world about health, well-being, exercise and nutrition but unless you understand 'you', what drives and motivates you, what your values are and how to incorporate these aspects into your life (in a meaningful way) it is difficult to make new habits stick.

Ideally we are looking for new habits to be automatic and for you to have the confidence to maintain changes in the future (after this programme finishes).

Also, it is worth noting that not everything is within our control. We have to consider psychology, physiology (and particularly gut health), our environment and our support network. We can also build some strategies to manage stressful times (when some things are out of our control).

Motivation:

People mention the 'M' word quite often. You might think that some people are naturally highly motivated and others, hmmm, not so much. I believe that for people to have a chance of success they would need to understand their goals, what achieving that goal means to them, how to get to the goal (by setting specific, smaller targets), that the goal is pitched correctly (i.e.: not too grand or far off into the future) and MOST IMPORTANTLY that the goal is in line with that person's values.

Behaviour Change – What, When, Why?

In this module you may recall that I asked you "What is important to me?" and you made a list of your reasons for starting this programme. I then asked you to visualise you at your very best following some deep breathing exercises.

"What type of person will you be in 6 months time?" I then asked you to work backwards and visualise yourself in 6 weeks, this week and today. Writing this down really helps you understand 'what' it is that you want to achieve.

Please revisit these questions before moving on.

Use this space to revisit the above questions.

"What are your reasons for starting this programme?"

In each weekly check in call, I ask my clients "What are your wins this week" and "What are your challenges?" It's worth looking back at the reports you are sent straight after the meeting, to remind yourself of these aspects (WGW – What's Going Well and EBI – Even Better If).

In a nutshell, if you are listing lots of WGWs then we might need to set a new goal and if you are listing lots of EBIs (challenges) then we discuss strategies or we might need to tweak the original goal.

Please revisit your latest goal.

Use this space to revisit your latest goal.

Habits:

We have two types: 'Healthy / Helpful' and 'Unhealthy / Unhelpful'. In your task today I am going to ask you to make a list of all those habits, in both categories, that you currently have in your wheelhouse.

For example (and these are a few compared to MANY):

Healthy / Helpful:

- Brushing your teeth
- Making the bed
- Walking the dog every morning
- Drinking water first thing in the morning, before coffee

Unhealthy / Unhelpful:

- At 11am reaching for a cuppa and a biscuit (not hungry)
- After dinner eating a dessert (convincing myself that I need something sweet)
- 6pm – Rewarding myself with a glass of wine when the day has gone well (and / or I am making dinner)
- 6pm – Commiserating with a glass of wine when the day has been crappy
- Friday night unhealthy takeaway

So how do we change?

It's not sensible to think that we must break these unhealthy habits and build great new ones all at once. It's also important to note that our habits (healthy and unhealthy) can provide intrinsic reward (i.e.: boredom, stress and hunger can result in us craving sugary foods / snacks). Any new healthy habit you want, especially to replace an unhealthy habit, will need to provide similar reward. Also understanding your thought process and steps (leading up to having / undertaking the unhealthy habit) allows you to at least make a rational decision such as "Do I really need this right now?"

Firstly, choose one (I would suggest the quick or easier win). For example, I suggest having a glass of water first thing in the morning. This isn't so hard but does require some cues (i.e.: a note by the sink, a glass beside the bed or a reminder in the phone). Most people can pick this habit up quite easily and the psychology geeks argue about how long it takes to cement (around 21 days) but I really like the approach by Matt Cutts (Google Engineer) and how he likes to set 30 day challenges. Revisit page 73.

Small changes = sustainable

Tasks to complete:

List Your Habits

For your task today I would like you to list your healthy and unhealthy habits and then choose one for the 30 day challenge.

Use this space to plan your 30 day challenge.

39

DAY THIRTY NINE

Changing Your Story

How changing your story can change your life

Think about a story that you are telling yourself right now. Who are the characters in the story? If you told your friends a story they would react in a 'I know what you want to hear' type way. If you told a professional or a stranger this story (completely impartial) what would they say? Lori describes an honest account as 'delivering compassionate truth bombs'!

Watch the video:
https://www.youtube.com/watch?v=O_MQr4lHm0c

Mint Chocolate Chip Ice Cream

2 servings
5 minutes

Ingredients

2 Banana (sliced and frozen)
1/4 cup Mint Leaves (chopped)
1 3/4 ozs Dark Chocolate (at least 70% cacao, roughly chopped)

Directions

1. Add frozen bananas and fresh mint to food processor and blend. Occasionally scrape down the sides and continue to blend until smooth (approximately 3 to 5 minutes).
2. Stir in the chopped chocolate.
3. Scoop into a bowl and enjoy immediately as soft serve or for firmer ice cream, place in an airtight, freezer-safe container and freeze for at least 1 hour before scooping.

Notes

Leftovers: Freeze in an airtight container for up to three months.
More Creamy: Add a splash of coconut milk.
More Scoopable: Add 1 tbsp vodka to prevent hard freeze.
Less Work: Skip the chopping and use dark chocolate chips instead.

DAY FORTY ONE

Did You Know?

Did you know that dietary fibre is hugely important to help keep you feeling fuller for longer, maintaining healthy blood fat levels and keeping the gut and other organs healthy? We don't digest fibre but it is necessary for our health.

DAY FORTY TWO

Day Off!

Book a FREE call with Gilly!

Enhance your progress with a FREE 15 minute consultation, simply see here to book:

https://p.bttr.to/2Ol0Aln

Join the community on social media:

@BetterNutritionby Gilly Facebook and Instagram

Weekly Reflection:

Think about what you have learnt this week and what resonates with you the most.

7

WELCOME TO

WEEK SEVEN

Week to Restore

It's time to chill. Yes, I mean switch off from this and forget it.

We've looked at stress. There will always be stressors and aspects of your own life which you find 'challenging'.

Here's the thing... stress produces cortisol.

Cortisol is a steroid hormone that regulates a wide range of processes throughout the body, including metabolism and the immune response. It also has a very important role in helping the body respond to stress. It's our fight or flight hormone and is very necessary when being chased by a tiger.

Stress is an adrenal hormone and helps us to run faster, see further, think clearer and hear better as well as pumping additional fuel into the body. It gives us quick energy when we are racing away from Timothy Tiger (Grrrrrrrrrr)! But, it also slows down metabolism and our digestion.

When we relax, the flow of blood increases around our body giving us more energy. It helps us to have a calmer and clearer mind, which aids positive thinking, concentration, memory and decision making. Relaxation slows our heart rate, reduces our blood pressure and relieves tension.

So, take this week off. I mean off EVERYTHING. Look at restoration. Yoga, massage, baths with candles, walking in nature, knitting, playing with kittens, doing a jigsaw, reading (not this eBook... I'm watching).

Tasks to complete:

Activity List

List the activities you would like to do this week to help your body and mind 'restore'.

Use this space to plan your 30 day challenge.

Book a FREE call with Gilly!

Enhance your progress with a FREE 15 minute consultation,
simply see here to book:
https://p.bttr.to/2Ol0AIn

Join the community on social media:

@BetterNutritionby Gilly Facebook and Instagram

8

WELCOME TO

WEEK EIGHT

Understanding Osteoporosis

Osteoporosis is not just a disease for the elderly. Not enough vitamins and minerals, too much fast food and a sedentary lifestyle can all mean that this disease, affecting our bones, can be developed earlier in life.

In 2017, NHS England reported:

In the UK over 3 million people are estimated to have osteoporosis and there are estimated to be over 500,000 fragility fractures that occur in the UK each year. Many of those fractures could be prevented with earlier identification and intervention.

This video gives a basic explanation about how osteoporosis occurs and what our amazing army of cells are doing to form and then restore our bones. The osteoblast cells are responsible for the formation of bone, and the osteoclast cells are responsible for the breakdown of bones. They are busily working away together.

According to NHS England, apart from poor diet and lack of exercise, the following factors may increase the risk of osteoporosis:

- taking high-dose steroid tablets for more than 3 months
- other medical conditions (inflammatory conditions, hormone-related conditions or malabsorption problems)
- a family history of osteoporosis (particularly a hip fracture in a parent)
- long-term use of certain medicines that can affect bone strength or hormone levels (e.g.: anti-oestrogen tablets that many women take after breast cancer)
- having or having had an eating disorder such as anorexia or bulimia
- having a low body mass index (BMI)
- heavy drinking and smoking

Women, the menopause and osteoporosis:

Oestrogen is a hormone that protects bones. Unfortunately, oestrogen decreases sharply when women reach menopause, which may lead to bone loss and the chance of developing osteoporosis. For this reason, women are more at risk of osteoporosis than men and, particularly, if the menopause begins early (before the age of 45) or they've had their ovaries removed.

How does nutrition help prevent the risk of osteoporosis?

Dietary proteins are key nutrients for bone health and thereby function in the prevention of osteoporosis. Protein intake affects bone in several ways:

1. Provides the structural matrix of bone.
2. Optimises insulin-like growth factor (IGF-1) levels – needed for normal bone and tissue growth / development.
3. May increase urinary calcium (indicating an increase of calcium absorption in the intestines).

Our bones also need the following minerals and vitamins and I have put some info in chart form to give more detail:

Minerals

	BENEFITS	RECOM-MENDED AMOUNT (NRVs)	UPPER LIMIT (UL) / day	GOOD FOOD SOURCES	DID YOU KNOW?
CALCIUM	Builds and protects bones and teeth. Helps with muscle contractions and relaxation, blood clotting, and nerve impulse transmission. Plays a role in hormone secretion and enzyme activation. Helps maintain healthy blood pressure	31–50yrs: M: 1,000 mg, W: 1,000 mg 51-70 yrs: M: 1,000 mg, W: 1,200 mg, 71+: M: 1,200 mg, W: 1,200 mg	2,500 mg	Yoghurt, cheese, milk, tofu, sardines, salmon, fortified juices, leafy green vegetables, such as broccoli and kale (but not spinach or Swiss chard, which have binders that lessen absorption)	Adults absorb roughly 30% of calcium ingested, but this can vary depending on the source. Diets very high in calcium may increase the risk of prostate cancer.
MAGNESIUM	Needed for many chemical reactions in the body. Works with calcium in muscle contraction, blood clotting, and regulation of blood pressure. Helps build bones and teeth	18+: M: 420 mg, W: 320 mg	350 mg (Note: This upper limit applies to supplements and medicines, such as laxatives, not to dietary magnesium).	Green vegetables such as spinach and broccoli, legumes, cashews, sunflower seeds and other seeds, halibut, whole-wheat bread, milk	The majority of magnesium in the body is found in bones. If your blood levels are low, your body may tap into these reserves to correct the problem.
PHOSPHORUS	Helps build and protect bones and teeth. Part of DNA and RNA. Helps convert food into energy. Part of phospholipids, which carry lipids in blood and help shuttle nutrients into and out of cells	M: 700 mg, W: 700 mg	31–70: 4,000 mg 71+: 3,000 mg	Wide variety of foods, including milk and dairy products, meat, fish, poultry, eggs, liver, green peas, broccoli, potatoes, almonds	Certain drugs bind with phosphorus, making it unavailable and causing bone loss, weakness, and pain.

Our bones also need the following minerals and vitamins and I have put some info in chart form to give more detail:

Vitamins

	BENEFITS	RECOM-MENDED AMOUNT (NRVs)	UPPER LIMIT (UL) / day	GOOD FOOD SOURCES	DID YOU KNOW?
RETINOIDS / CAROTENE (Vit A; includes retinol, retinal, retinyl esters, and retinoic acid). These are also referred to as "preformed" Vit A. Beta carotene can easily be converted to vitamin A as needed.	Essential for vision. Lycopene may lower prostate cancer risk. Keeps tissues and skin healthy. Plays an important role in bone growth and in the immune system. Diets rich in the carotenoids alpha carotene and lycopene seem to lower lung cancer risk. Carotenoids act as antioxidants. Foods rich in the carotenoids lutein and zeaxanthin may protect against cataracts	M: 900 mcg (3,000 IU) W: 700 mcg (2,333 IU) Some supplements report Vit A in international units (IUs).	3,000 mcg (about 10,000 IU)	Sources of retinoids: beef liver, eggs, shrimp, fish, fortified milk, butter, cheddar cheese, Swiss cheese Sources of beta carotene: sweet potatoes, carrots, pumpkins, squash, spinach, mangoes, turnip greens	People may get too much preformed vitamin A from food and supplements. Large amounts of supplemental vitamin A (but not beta carotene) can be harmful to bones.
CALCIFEROL (Vit D)	Helps maintain normal blood levels of calcium and phosphorus, which strengthen bones. Helps form teeth and bones. Supplements can reduce the number of non-spinal fractures	31–70: 15 mcg (600 IU) 71+: 20 mcg (800 IU)	50 mcg (2,000 IU)	Fortified milk or margarine, fortified cereals, fatty fish	Many people don't get enough of this nutrient. While the body uses sunlight to make vitamin D, it cannot make enough if you live in northern climates or don't spend much time in the sun.

How does exercise help with osteoporosis?

Regular activity reduces the rate of bone loss and conserves bone tissue. Bone adapts by building more cells and becoming more dense each time we exercise, which then lowers the risk of fractures. Exercise also helps reduce the risk of falling by increasing balance and coordination skills.

If you would like more information about what exercise is beneficial for bone strengthening then have a look at the Royal Osteoporosis Society website: https://theros.org.uk/information-and-support/osteoporosis/living-with-osteoporosis/exercise-and-physical-activity-for-osteoporosis/bone-and-muscle-strengthening/

The Royal Osteoporosis Society also have a good fact sheet on exercises to promote bone strength, click here to view: https://strwebstgmedia.blob.core.windows.net/media/z2mhsbs2/exercises-to-promote-bone-and-muscle-strength-fact-sheet-february-2019.pdf

Dark Chocolate Peanut Butter Cups

10 servings

1 hour 15 minutes

Ingredients

5 1/4 ozs Dark Chocolate (at least 70% cacao, broken into pieces)
1 1/2 tbsps Coconut Oil
1/2 cup All Natural Peanut Butter
1/2 tsp Vanilla Extract
1/8 tsp Sea Salt

Directions

1. Arrange paper baking cups on a plate or a small baking sheet. Set aside.
2. Set up a double boiler: Fill a medium pot with an inch of water and place a smaller pot or heat-safe bowl on top ensuring the water is not touching the bottom of the smaller pot or bowl. The smaller pot or bowl should rest tightly on top of the pot and any water or steam should not be able to escape.
3. Bring water to a boil then reduce to lowest heat. Add the dark chocolate and coconut oil to the smaller pot and stir until melted. Remove from heat.
4. Divide half of the melted chocolate between the paper baking cups. There should be a thin, even layer of chocolate in each baking cup. Freeze for 10 to 15 minutes until solid.
5. Meanwhile, in a bowl combine the peanut butter, vanilla and salt. Stir until smooth.
6. Divide the peanut butter between the baking cups by spooning the peanut butter into the center of solid chocolate. Drizzle the remaining melted dark chocolate around and overtop the peanut butter.
7. Return to the freezer for about 30 minutes or until solid. Enjoy!

Notes

Leftovers: Refrigerate in an airtight container for up to one week or freeze for up to one month. Peanut Butter Cups will melt if stored at room temperature.

Serving Size: One serving is one peanut butter cup.

Nut-Free: Use sunflower seed butter instead.

Nutrient Cycling

If you've heard of the phrase nutrient cycling but still feel at a bit of a loss as to what it actually means, you're far from alone. The term is being flung around the fitness industry more frequently than HIIT (High Intensity Interval Training) and EPOC (Excess Post-Exercise Oxygen Consumption – aka how to burn calories fast).

But what is it? A new nutrition approach preaching how to eat healthy, another crazy diet fad or simply an alternate way to approach your fueling? *Women's Health* interviewed me a few years ago to understand the basics of eating around your workouts.

Your Step by Step Guide

1. Plan your weekly training

The whole point of nutrient cycling is that you are adequately fuelling your engine before, and refuelling after, each session, so you'll need to plan your workouts in advance. Remember, achieving your body / health goals doesn't just happen (you have to think, plan, execute and reflect).

2. Training in the morning

Make sure you fuel up the evening before with adequate protein, carbs and fat. That way, you'll have enough energy banked to do your workout faster in the morning. Then refuel with carbs and protein as soon as you can after training. A clean protein powder spooned into overnight oats is a quick win.

3. Training at lunchtime

If you want to keep it simple, the rule of thumb would be avoid fat for one-two hours pre and post workout (regardless whether that's before breakfast, lunch or evening). You do need to get your macronutrients in during the day but, if you're having three meals a day, you'll be getting your macronutrients right throughout the day anyway.

If you do an easy lunchtime session, It's good to get your protein and carbohydrates in within a 45 minute window. Then, if you're hungry a few hours after that, have a snack that includes all three macronutrients, including fat.

4. Training in the evening

Eat a breakfast based on protein, carbs and fat, such as salmon with scrambled eggs on toasted rye bread, followed by a lunch which omits carbs and finally a dinner (post workout) made up of all the macros, including carbs, as they're necessary to replenish your energy stores.

5. If you don't have a routine

Don't worry, you can still keep track. You always know by the night before, so get a training diary and note down before bed when you're going to train. This way, you know when you need to fuel.

6. Play by the (basic) rules

There's no point nutrient cycling around a poor diet. Try to get plenty of sleep, rehydrate regularly and don't rush your meals. Toxins like alcohol will harm results, so note down 'if and when' you indulge. Which, if you're bothering with all this, should probably be less, rather than more, often.

Just to reiterate, you should be realistic about how well you are doing with the basics (3 meals per day with the right portions of protein, carbs, fats and veggies / greens / colours, consistently) before worrying about cutting out food groups around training. This is getting more 'specific' and can be counterproductive. If you are happy with the feedback you've had on your Food / Mood Journals then this is something to ask about on your next Weekly Catch-Up call.

Tasks to complete:

Nutrient Cycling

If this is the 'next step' for you (and your basic three meals per day have been 'on point') then feel free to make a plan here. Firstly, list the days you are exercising (don't worry about day-to-day activities such as dog walking and gardening, etc.). Secondly, plan your meals and food groups around your training sessions.

	Training Y / N	Break-fast	Training Y / N	Lunch	Training Y / N	Dinner	Training Y / N	Supper	Training Y / N
M									
T									
W									
T									
F									
S									
S									

Why Is Sleep Important?

So you might wonder why a nutritionist also considers sleep, stress and other lifestyle factors? Well, most lifestyle factors are linked to our health, associated diseases and our weight management. Sleep as well as our genetics, stress levels, exercise habits and other health considerations can create a delicious or damaging cocktail!

Whilst poor sleep isn't the only factor associated with weight gain, it is something to be considered. It doesn't take much sleep deprivation to increase an individual's weight. There have been studies which show that in one week of poor sleep participants gained 2 pounds each, on average.

Now, if you are a new mum or have nocturnal pets, work shifts or are going through the menopause (suffering from night sweats, etc.) then obviously, getting the 'perfect' night's sleep may be more challenging, but there are some strategies which you can at least try and put in place to improve the situation.

Why does a lack of sleep cause weight gain? This is down to multiple changes in our bodies and our hormones seem to be affected the most. Leptin is our 'fullness' hormone, which works hand in hand with ghrelin, which is our 'hunger' hormone. When we lack sleep, leptin is suppressed and ghrelin is triggered and increases.

Now, we are all individual and will need differing amounts of sleep but assume that 7-9 hours per night is the recommended amount.

In a nutshell – why is good sleep important?:

- Our bodies and minds recover from the previous day
- Helps to lose body fat and keep us lean
- Maintains our overall happiness
- Allows our hormones to reset (essential for weight loss, muscle build or weight maintenance)
- Allows us to maintain mental focus
- Keeps us healthy!

Suffering as a person who 'just doesn't sleep well' shouldn't be a thing. You can check your sleep protocol and make sure you're at least aware of your before bed routine (and if this might be having a negative effect) and also your environment (which can be changed). We can always improve situations. We should be ever-evolving.

HOW MANY HOURS OF SLEEP DO YOU GET?									
1	2	3	4	5	6	7	8	9	10

HOW WOULD YOU RATE THE QUALITY OF YOUR SLEEP?									
1	2	3	4	5	6	7	8	9	10

Here are some tips outside of the bedroom:

- Determine your regular pattern of times for going to bed and waking up (try writing this down in list form).
- Avoid drinking too much water in the period 2-3 hours before bedtime to avoid having to nip to the loo during the night.
- Avoid stimulants such as caffeine from midday (this includes tea)!
- Even 1 alcoholic drink in the evening can disrupt sleep quantity and quality.
- Avoid the use of blue light (i.e.: laptops, smartphones, TV and tablets) one hour before your set bedtime.
- Avoid large meals 2-3 hours before bedtime.
- Take a teaspoon (small portion) of healthy fats before bed (something like peanut butter), which produce relatively slow increases in blood glucose and modest insulin release.
- If you work at a desk all day or sit in your car / van then it is beneficial to stretch out before going to bed.
- Avoid high sugar foods and drinks a couple of hours before bed.
- Before bed, have a shower or bath to help de-stress and allow the warm water to relax you.
- Clear your mind. It can help to keep a pencil and pad next to the bed so you can offload anything on your mind, 'parking' it and picking it up the next day. It also helps if you create lists of 'to do' and include your meals, preparation time, shopping and activity, etc.
- Regular exercise works to fatigue your muscles as well as your mind and aids in hormone balance. This helps make you physically tired as well as mentally. However, avoid exercising too close to bedtime as this ramps up your Central Nervous System (CNS), making it difficult to switch off.
- Practise common relaxation techniques such as deep breathing (there are good apps, such as 'Breathe' and 'HeadSpace').
- Read positive articles or books before bed to calm your mind (nothing like *Schindler's List*)!
- Work with your circadian rhythms. As a species we should sleep when it's dark and wake up when it's light. Try not to fight this.

Use these tips inside the bedroom:

- Create a relaxing sleep area, quiet and peaceful.
- Ensure the room you sleep in is as dark as possible (use blackout shades / roller blinds and curtains).
- Cover small sources of light (e.g.: digital clocks).
- Look to keep your bedroom relatively organised, avoiding clutter on bedside cabinets and floors, etc.
- Aim for a cool room temperature.
- If noise is an issue, investigate the use of a sleep machine or white noise generator, which help to mask sounds.
- Aim to wake up in your light sleep phase rather than deep sleep phase.
- Use a progressive volume alarm clock to gently bring you out of your sleep rather than Iron Maiden blasting out!
- Have a glass of water beside the bed for use overnight or on waking.

The bottom line is that good sleep is crucial for good health and so quality sleep should be a priority as your physical, mental and emotional health depend on it.

Paleo Granola

8 servings

40 minutes

Ingredients

1 cup Slivered Almonds
1 cup Sunflower Seeds
1/2 cup Pumpkin Seeds
1 cup Unsweetened Coconut Flakes
1/4 cup Ground Flax Seed
1/4 cup Coconut Oil (melted)
1/2 cup Sunflower Seed Butter
1/4 cup Raw Honey
1/2 tsp Sea Salt
1 tsp Cinnamon
1 cup Dried Unsweetened Cranberries
2 cups Unsweetened Almond Milk

Directions

1. Preheat the oven to 300°F (149°C). Line a large baking sheet with parchment paper.
2. Combine all ingredients except the dried cranberries and almond milk together in a large mixing bowl. Mix very well until all ingredients are evenly distributed. Using your hands works best! Spread the mixture evenly across the baking sheet.
3. Bake for 30 minutes, giving a stir at the 15 minute mark.
4. Remove from oven and let cool completely. Once cool, transfer into a mixing bowl and add dried cranberries. Toss well to evenly distribute.
5. Add to a bowl and serve with a bit of almond milk for breakfast or eat dry as a snack. Enjoy!

Notes

Storage: Store in a mason jar or airtight container in the fridge for up to 1 week.
Serving Size: One serving is roughly 3/4 cup of granola.
Nut Allergy: Use sesame seeds instead of slivered almonds.
No Dried Cranberries: Use raisins.

DAY FIFTY FIVE

Did You Know?

Did you know that statistically, more people who set short term goals and check in with a coach, friend or family member are more likely to succeed on a weight loss program? Set your goals realistically.

DAY FIFTY SIX

Day Off!

Book a FREE Discovery Call:

https://p.bttr.to/312Scn1

Join the community on social media:
@BetterNutritionby Gilly Facebook and Instagram

Weekly Reflection:

Think about what you have learnt this week and what resonates with you the most.

9

WELCOME TO

WEEK NINE

57

DAY FIFTY SEVEN

Sleep is Your Super Power

Sleep is Your Superpower

Sleep is your life-support system and Mother Nature's best effort yet at immortality, says sleep scientist Matt Walker. Learn more about sleep's impact on your learning, memory, immune system and even your genetic code as well as some helpful tips for improving sleep quality and quantity.

Watch the video:
https://www.ted.com/talks/matt_walker_sleep_is_your_superpower?language=en

Golden Turmeric Hot Chocolate

1 serving
5 minutes

Ingredients

1 tbsp Cacao Powder
1/4 tsp Turmeric (dried, ground)
1/4 tsp Cinnamon
1 1/2 tsps Coconut Butter
1/2 tsp Honey
1 cup Water (hot)
1/2 cup Unsweetened Almond Milk

Directions

1 Add the cacao powder, turmeric, cinnamon, coconut butter, honey, hot water and almond milk to a blender. Blend on high until smooth and creamy. Transfer to a mug and enjoy!

Notes

No Cacao Powder: Use cocoa powder instead.
No Honey: Use maple syrup or stevia instead.
Nut-Free: Use oat milk or coconut milk instead.
No Coconut Butter: Use almond, cashew or sunflower seed butter instead.

Lifestyle and Hypertension

Most people are aware that salt should be avoided for anyone with high blood pressure but there are considerations for EVERYONE as we cannot see what is happening inside our arteries; for every poor choice we make it is possible we could be affecting our circulatory system.

Hypertension is not an 'age' disease. The NHS report:

Over 2.1 million people under the age of 45 had high blood pressure in England in 2015.

Globally – after poor diet, high blood pressure is the second biggest known risk factor for disease.

UK – after smoking and poor diet, high blood pressure is the third biggest risk factor for disease.

Cardiovascular disease and related disability – high blood pressure is the largest, single known risk factor and increases the risk of heart failure, coronary artery disease and stroke. High blood pressure can also increase the risk of chronic kidney disease, peripheral arterial disease and vascular dementia.

Blood Pressure Ranges

Blood pressure (BP classification (Williams *et al.* 2004; NICE, 2011)		
Category	Systolic BP (mmHg)	Diastolic BP (mmHg)
Optimal blood pressure	>120	>80
Normal blood pressure	>130	>85
High normal blood pressure	130-139	85–89
Stage 1 Hypertension	140–159	90–99
Stage 2 Hypertension	160–179	100–109
Severe Hypertension	≥180	≥110

The NHS list increased risk factors as:

- you are over the age of 65
- are overweight
- are of African or Caribbean descent
- have a relative with high blood pressure
- eat too much salt
- do not eat enough fruit and vegetables
- do not do enough exercise
- drink too much alcohol or coffee (or other caffeine-based drinks)
- smoke
- do not get much sleep or have disturbed sleep

These healthy lifestyle modifications can significantly reduce your risk of hypertension:

Lifestyle modifications to prevent and manage hypertension	
Lifestyle modification	Approximate systolic blood pressure lowering (mmHg) (Aronow *et al.* 2011)
Lose weight if overweight or obese	5–20/10kg weight loss
Reduce sodium intake to <6g of salt/day	2–8
Limit alcohol consumption to <3 units/day for men and <2 units/day for women Less advisable if overweight Binge drinking must be avoided	2–4
Take regular aerobic physical exercise Ideally for >30 minutes/day on at least 5 days/week Consume at least five portions/day of fruit and vegetables	4–9
DASH diet	8–14

The chart above is the perfect example of how hypertension and the systolic blood pressure measure can be lowered. Let's look at an individual with a blood pressure measure of 159 / 99.

After following the protocols their measures would read as follows:

1. Low salt diet, consistently (systolic BP reading down to approximately 152)
2. Reduce weight by 10kg (systolic BP reading down to 139)
3. Regular exercise (systolic BP reading down to 132)
4. Ensuring 5 portions of veggies / fruit per day (systolic BP reading down to 122)
5. Reduce alcohol consumption (systolic reading down to 120)

This is an example of how lifestyle measures can lower an individual's blood pressure to a normal range. Please note that this is not 'absolute' and every individual will have different readings and reductions, responding better to some interventions than others.

Please note (again) that you might not be currently classed as having hypertension but when looking at the modifiable risk factors you may be able to improve or change some lifestyle factors and reduce your BP to an even better range.

Tasks to complete:

Check Your Blood Pressure

If you haven't had it checked for a while then your local pharmacy can check it.

Use this space to record your blood pressure.

What Do Vegan / Vegetarians Need?

There is no doubt that consuming more plants in our diet is beneficial (I discussed this in the Fibre module) and being vegetarian, vegan or flexitarian is healthy for the body and our planet. However, these approaches should consider vitamins, minerals and amino acids, which may be lacking unless understood and planned into a daily / weekly meal plan.

Vegan / Veggie Iron:

Iron is essential for the production of red blood cells. Haemoglobin is the substance in red blood cells that carries oxygen from your lungs to transport it throughout your body. Haemoglobin represents about two-thirds of the body's iron. If you don't have enough iron, your body can't make enough healthy oxygen-carrying red blood cells.

Two-thirds of the women in the world are iron deficient and so it is even more important that dietary iron is a regular visitor in our diets.

A vegan diet can be high in iron, although iron from plant-based food (non-heme) is absorbed by the body less well than iron from animal sources (heme).

Good sources of iron for vegans are:

- pulses
- wholemeal bread and flour
- breakfast cereals fortified with iron
- dark green, leafy vegetables, such as watercress, broccoli and spring greens
- nuts
- dried fruits, such as apricots, prunes and figs

Vegetarian / Vegan – Amino Acids (AAs)

AAs are compounds that combine to make proteins. When a person eats a food that contains protein, their digestive system breaks the protein down into AAs. The body then combines the AAs in various ways to carry out bodily functions.

AAs build muscle, cause chemical reactions in the body, transport nutrients, prevent illness and carry out other functions. AA deficiency can result in decreased immunity, digestive problems, depression, fertility issues, lower mental alertness, slowed growth in children, and many other health issues.

The body needs 20 different AAs to maintain good health and normal functioning (crucial strength of the body, hair, skin, organs and just about everything else). A protein healthy diet is beneficial in the right amounts.. People must obtain nine of these essential amino acids, through food. Dietary sources of amino acids can come from animal products (e.g.: meat, fish, seafood, poultry, eggs and dairy, etc.) AND also available for those following a plant-based approach (tofu, soy, buckwheat and quinoa etc.).

A healthy body can manufacture the other 11 AAs, so these do not usually need to enter the body through the diet. They are non-essential AAs.

Each of the essential AAs plays a different role in the body, and the symptoms of deficiency vary accordingly.

The branched-chain amino acids (BCAAs), isoleucine, leucine and valine, are essential amino acids (EAAs) that may enhance the response of muscle to exercise.

Amino Acid	Main Food Sources
Histidine	soy protein, eggs, parmesan, sesame, peanuts
Isoleucine	eggs, soy protein & tofu, white fish, pork, parmesan
Leudine	eggs, soy protein , white fish, parmesan, sesame
Lysine	eggs, soy protein , white fish, parmesan, smelts
Methionine	eggs, white fish, sesame, smelts, soy protein
Cysteine	eggs, soy protein, sesame, mustard seeds, peanuts
Phenylalanine	eggs, soy protein, peanuts, sesame, white fish
Tyrosine	soy protein, eggs, parmesan, peanuts, sesame
Threonine	eggs, soy protein, white fish, smelts, sesame
Tryptophan	soy protein, sesame, eggs, winged beans, chia seeds
Valine	eggs, soy protein, parmesan, sesame, beef

Vegan / Veggie Vitamin B12

The body needs vitamin B12 to maintain healthy blood and a healthy nervous system. Many people get vitamin B12 from animal sources, such as meat, fish and dairy products. Sources for vegans are limited and a vitamin B12 supplement may be needed.

Sources of vitamin B12 for vegans include:

- breakfast cereals fortified with B12
- unsweetened soya drinks fortified with vitamin B12
- yeast extract, such as Marmite, which is fortified with vitamin B12

Vegan / Veggie Calcium

Calcium is needed for strong and healthy bones and teeth. Non-vegans get most of their calcium from dairy foods (milk, cheese and yoghurt), but vegans / veggies can get it from other foods.

Good sources of calcium for vegans include:

- green, leafy vegetables – such as broccoli, cabbage and okra, but not spinach
- fortified unsweetened soya, rice and oat drinks
- calcium-set tofu
- sesame seeds and tahini
- pulses
- brown and white bread (in the UK, calcium is added to white and brown flour by law)
- dried fruit, such as raisins, prunes, figs and dried apricots

Vegan / Veggie Vitamin D

The body needs Vitamin D to regulate the amount of calcium and phosphate in the body. These nutrients help keep bones, teeth and muscles healthy.

Good sources of vitamin D for vegans / veggies include:

- exposure to sunlight, particularly from late March / early April to the end of September – remember to cover up or protect your skin before it starts to turn red or burn
- fortified fat spreads, breakfast cereals and unsweetened soya drinks (with Vitamin D added)
- Vitamin D supplements

**Read the label to ensure the vitamin D used in a product is not of animal origin.

Tasks to complete:

Choose a Meal

Consider choosing a meal this week and trialling either:

a) more plants

b) something different / new

c) a pure veggie / vegan option

Use this space to plan your meal.

A)

B)

C)

Raspberry Chia Breakfast Parfait

2 servings
15 minutes

Ingredients

1 cup Unsweetened Almond Milk
2 tbsps Chia Seeds
1 tsp Cinnamon
1 Banana (sliced)
1/2 cup Almonds (crushed)
2 tbsps Hemp Seeds
1/2 cup Raspberries

Directions

1. Mix almond milk, chia seeds and cinnamon in a bowl. Let sit for 10 - 20 minutes or until the milk has become a thick jelly. Transfer into jars (depending on how many servings you are making).

2. Next add banana onto the milk/chia seed layer. Then add almonds followed by hemp hearts. Top with raspberries and enjoy!

DAY SIXTY TWO

Did You Know?

Did you know that anxiety and depression can be positively assisted through exercise and a change in nutrition? Just by taking small steps you can improve your mental well-being.

DAY SIXTY THREE

Day Off!

Book a FREE Discovery Call:

https://p.bttr.to/312Scn1

Join the community on social media:

@BetterNutritionby Gilly Facebook and Instagram

Weekly Reflection:

Think about what you have learnt this week and what resonates with you the most.

10

WELCOME TO

WEEK TEN

Your Personal Values

Goals focus on the outcome (e.g.: get healthier by increasing my vegetable consumption, 5-7 days per week). As a result and as we achieve them or change our viewpoint goals change. It's important to view our progress with goals regularly.

Values provide guidance. They define how we continue to live. They are the glue that keep us together and are more consistent. They connect us to a greater purpose in life. They differentiate the important from the unimportant. They are a 'non-negotiable' source of motivation and energy.

Without understanding your values and why these are important to you it is difficult to make some goals stick. The two are connected. Why should I increase my consumption of vegetables if health isn't one of my values?

I like the explanation in the first half of this video by Jan Stasson: https://www.youtube.com/watch?v=_a1Fc6nwpks

You can create understanding and context by adding a story next to your values. Jan set up The Museum of Values and suggests adding a story to each of our chosen values. If you were telling this story about 'respect', 'friendship', 'compassion', 'love' then you would be reminded of, and can explain why, these values are important.

For example: Why is tenacity one of my goals? I grew up watching my parents work extremely hard, moving hundreds of miles and away from their family and friends to achieve a better salary and life for us. They then owned two businesses through some pretty hard times. I witnessed my mum working 3 jobs when my parents got divorced. So I feel, for me, there is only working hard and moving forwards even in difficult circumstances.

That is a story connected to one of my core values – tenacity. If I can tell this story to my partner, my friends and colleagues then they understand why hard work and tenacity are important to me (and maybe why I get frustrated with my partner when he is on a 14-hour sofa / rugby watching 'doom and gloom' or "I'm bored" day). This is why I snap "Get up (NOW) and find something worthwhile to do which will make you feel some achievement"!

Think about your values:

Try searching for your values. Here are 100 examples and a description: https://liveboldandbloom.com/05/values/list-of-values

Getting used to describing your values and how these link to your goals is also important and useful. This is how you can link the drive with the reason and action. You can also justify your choices to people (i.e.: anyone trying to derail you or question your choices). These values can also help to motivate us and act as reinforcement for our choices.

For example: I really value healthy eating so that I am a role model to my family. I am currently following a healthy nutrition and lifestyle programme. My goals are to 'X' in 'Y' time by following some nutritional recommendations, uploading my meal choices and (you get my drift).

Can you write a sentence using one of your chosen values and how this relates to your participation in this programme? What are you goals and how do these help you feel as though you're working towards the right 'stuff'?

Use this space to pinpoint the TRULY important aspects of your life.

Almond Butter & Jam Chia Pudding

2 servings
30 minutes

Ingredients

1/4 cup Chia Seeds
1 cup Unsweetened Almond Milk
1 cup Raspberries
2 tbsps Almond Butter

Directions

1. In a medium bowl, combine the chia seeds with the almond milk and whisk well, making sure all the seeds are incorporated. Refrigerate for at least 20 minutes or overnight to thicken.
2. In a small bowl, mash the raspberries until they resemble jam.
3. Layer the chia seed pudding in a jar, top with the raspberry jam and almond butter. Serve and enjoy!

Notes

Leftovers: Refrigerate covered for up to five days.
Nut-Free: Use coconut milk instead of almond milk. Use sunflower seed butter instead of almond butter.
More Protein: Add a scoop of protein powder to the milk mixture before setting. Whisk to fully incorporate with the seeds and milk.
Additional Toppings: Add cacao nibs for crunch.

66

DAY SIXTY SIX

Why Values Matter

Jan Stassen is the co-founder of the Museum of Values. After working in the field of advertising for many years, Jan became interested in social businesses and impact-driven initiatives. Out of his personal desire and frustration in advertising, he started reflecting on his own values and focusing on what is actually important to him. This internal journey led him to create the Museum of Values.

Click here to watch the video:
https://www.youtube.com/watch?v=_a1Fc6nwpks

Prevention of Chronic Diseases

Diet, Nutrition and the Prevention of Chronic Diseases

Because of changes in our diet and lifestyle patterns, chronic 'Non-Communicable Diseases' (NCDs) have been increasing over the past two decades. These are diseases which we do not 'catch' but instead are brought on by ourselves, through our lifestyle choices. Chronic diseases that are not sudden (acute) but those that develop over time and are preventable.

NCDs include obesity, diabetes mellitus, cardiovascular disease (CVD), hypertension, stroke and some cancers. NCDs increase disability and premature death, which also places an additional financial strain on our NHS.

Nutrition is now regarded as a major cause of chronic disease with scientific evidence increasingly supporting the view that changes in diet have strong effects (positive and negative) on health throughout our lives. Most importantly, dietary adjustments may not only influence present health, but may determine whether an individual will develop such diseases in later life (i.e.: cancer, cardiovascular disease and diabetes).

The experts' key findings included:

Obesity:

The imbalance between declining energy expenditure due to physical inactivity and high energy in the diet (excess calories whether from sugar, starches or fat) is the main determinant of the obesity epidemic. Increasing physical activity, plus reducing intakes of foods high in fat and foods and drinks high in sugars, can prevent unhealthy weight gain. Taking these simple goals to concrete action requires major social and environmental changes in order to effectively promote and support healthier choices at the individual level.

Diabetes:

Excess weight gain, overweight and obesity and physical inactivity account for the escalating rates of type 2 diabetes, worldwide. Diabetes leads to increased risk of heart disease, kidney disease, stroke and infections. Increased physical activity and maintaining a healthy weight play critical roles in the prevention and treatment of diabetes.

Cardiovascular diseases:

Cardiovascular diseases are the major killers worldwide. These are due to unbalanced diets and physical inactivity. Risk of their main forms (heart disease and stroke) is reduced by eating less trans-fats and saturated fats in moderation whilst consuming sufficient amounts of monounsaturated and polyunsaturated fats, vegetables and fruits (in moderation). Other positive factors are physical activity and maintaining a healthy weight. A reduction of salt intake helps reduce blood pressure, a major cause of cardiovascular diseases.

Cancer:

Tobacco is the number one cause of cancer but dietary factors contribute significantly to some types of cancer. Maintaining a healthy weight will reduce the risk for cancers of the oesophagus, colorectum, breast, endometrium and kidney. Limiting alcohol intake will reduce risk for cancers of the mouth, throat, oesophagus, liver and breast. Ensuring an adequate intake of vegetables and fruits (in moderation) should further reduce risk for oral cavity, oesophagus, stomach and colorectal cancer.

Osteoporosis and bone fractures:

Fragility fractures are a problem of older people. Adequate intakes of calcium (500 mg per day or more) and of vitamin D in populations with high osteoporosis rates helps to reduce fracture risk as well as sun exposure and physical activity to strengthen bones and muscles.

To summarise:

The crucial role of physical activity as part of nutrition and health is well known. Measures and policies required to promote healthier food consumption patterns and facilitate a physically active life share common grounds and are mutually interactive in determining healthier behaviours.

Healthy diets and physical activity are key to good nutrition and necessary for a long and healthy life. Eating nutrient dense foods and balancing energy intake with the necessary physical activity to maintain a healthy weight is essential at all stages of life. Unbalanced consumption of foods high in energy (sugar, starch and / or fat) and low in essential nutrients contributes to energy excess, overweight and obesity. The amount of the energy consumed in relation to physical activity and the quality of food are key determinants of nutrition related chronic disease.

Not all fats are the same and it pays to know the difference. People should eat less high-calorie foods, especially foods high in trans-fats, whilst consuming saturated fat in moderation. Sugar reduction is another key factor along with being physically active; choosing unsaturated fat and reducing salt; enjoying vegetables and legumes and selecting more plant and marine foods. This consumption pattern is not only healthier but more favourable to the environment and sustainable development.

Tasks to complete:

Make Health Your Priority

Consider today how incredibly healthy you may be if you managed to eat, consistently, three balanced meals per day in the right portions, did regular activity and regularly reviewed your sleep and stress strategies / protocols. Nothing to do with this task other than to think about the **BETTER** version of your current self that you **WILL** become. Prioritise you and your health (your loved ones will thank you for it).

Yogurt & Berries

2 servings

5 minutes

Ingredients

2 cups Plain Greek Yogurt

2 cups Frozen Berries (thawed)

Directions

1 Divide yogurt into glasses or bowls. Top with thawed frozen fruit. (Do the reverse if you like the fruit on the bottom.) Enjoy!

Notes

Dairy-Free: Use a dairy-free yogurt like coconut, almond or cashew.

No Frozen Berries: Use any type of fresh fruit instead.

DAY SIXTY NINE

Did You Know?

Stress comes from our thoughts and is a 'perception of a real or imagined threat to your body or ego'. If it is only perception then it isn't 'real'.

It's memories we have from the past and us 'guessing the outcome / future' which combine to create the 'perception'. If we didn't believe every silly thought that we had we would be more 'zen' and less likely to hold onto or gain weight. This is because cortisol affects our metabolic pathways.

DAY SEVENTY

Day Off!

Weekly Reflection:

Think about what you have learnt this week and what resonates with you the most.

11

WELCOME TO

WEEK ELEVEN

Fats in Food Vs Fats in the Body

We have three types of fat in the body – Visceral (around the abdomen, sitting beside the internal organs), subcutaneous (directly under the skin) and fat in the liver (steatosis).

Fat could be considered as an organ that interacts with your environment and helps maintain homeostasis within your body. Fat controls and modulates your fertility, your appetite and your mood. Your immune response will not work properly if you don't have the right amount of fat.

- The NHS report a big increase in 'Non Alcoholic Fatty Liver Disease' (NAFLD). This is caused by a build-up of fat in the liver. It's usually seen in people who are overweight or obese.
- A healthy liver should contain little or no fat. It's estimated up to 1 in every 3 people in the UK has early stages of NAFLD where there are small amounts of fat in their liver.
- NAFLD can lead to serious liver damage, including cirrhosis (where the liver shrinks and becomes scarred and lumpy). This damage is permanent and can lead to liver failure and cancer.
- Having high levels of fat in your liver is also associated with an increased risk of serious health problems, such as diabetes and kidney disease.
- Non-alcoholic steatohepatitis (NASH) is a more serious form of NAFLD where the liver has become inflamed (present in approximately 5% of the UK population).

Why we need dietary fat:

- Brain health (cognitive thinking)
- Improved memory and recall
- May aid weight loss
- Build cell membranes
- Sheaves surrounding our nerves
- Alzeimers
- T2DM
- HD – CVD
- Immune health
- Organ health
- Balancing hormones
- Improve blood glucose measures
- Aids absorption of vitamins (ADEK)
- Increase HDL – helps remove other forms of cholesterol from the bloodstream
- Decreases inflammation
- Blood clotting
- Muscle movement
- Satiety

The very old fashioned dietary recommendation in the UK was to follow a low fat diet. However, the Seven Countries' study (Finland, Greece, US, Italy, Yugoslavia, Netherlands and Japan) investigated links between coronary heart disease mortality and lifestyle factors, especially the intake of saturated fatty acids. This study found that Greece (in fact Crete) had the best diet and mortality rates, with lower numbers of heart disease, even though they consumed a higher fat diet: https://www.ncbi.nlm.nih.gov/pmc/articles/PMC2790142/#:~:text=The%20Seven%20Countries'%20study%20included,intake%20of%20saturated%20fatty%20acids

"This diet is consisting of a lot of fruit and vegetables, lots of fish, less salt and sugar, more unrefined cereals, beans and nuts. Going from a general notion of Mediterranean food to testing that food in clinical settings and testing nutrients as preventative agents, we can conclude that a generally healthy lifestyle, including a healthy diet, appropriate amounts of physical activity, good sleep and less stress, is the way to a heart healthy life".

Mediterranean (Cruetes) type diet:

- Dietary fat olive oil and Canola-based margarine
- Mainly monounsaturated / high oleic (fatty acid that occurs naturally in various animal and vegetable fats and oils)
- Mainly polyunsaturated / alphalinolenic (n-3) acids (ALA – seeds and oils).
- Omega ratio: n-3 / n-6 ratio of 1 / 5
- Wide variety of vegetables and fruits (high dietary antioxidants)
- Moderate intake of chicken, fish and wine

Why do we have fats in food?

- Look better
- Taste better
- Extend the shelf life and storage
- Improve the nutritional composition of a product (e.g. increase the vitamin content, e.g. by adding ascorbic acid)
- Aid the processing and manufacture (e.g. emulsifiers, to help mix together ingredients).

In a nutshell, to give the body the fats it needs to be healthy, to maintain a healthy weight and to avoid NAFLD follow:

CHOOSE SMALL AMOUNTS OF: Foods high in unsaturated fats	**EAT LESS OF:** Foods high in saturated fats and trans fats
Monounsaturated fats • Oils: rapeseed, olive, avocado, rice bran • Nuts: almonds, hazelnut, peanuts, cashew, macadamia, pistachio • Avocados • Margarine spreads	**Saturated fats** • Butter • Ghee / coconut / palm • Lard / tallow / cooking fat / suet • Visible meat fat: chicken skin, chops • Meat pies / sausages / corned beef • Cream / sour cream / cream cheese
Polyunsaturated fats • Oils: sunflower, corn, soya • Nuts and seeds: walnut, pinenut, brazil, linseed, pumpkin, sesame, sunflower • Oily fish (rich in omega-3s): pilchards mackerel, salmon, sardines, herring	**Trans fats** • Commercially baked or fried goods e.g. biscuits, crackers, pastries, cakes • "Partially hydrogenated vegetable oil" • Takeaways and processed foods

15 Minute Shrimp & Cabbage Stir Fry

2 servings

15 minutes

Ingredients

2 tbsps Coconut Oil (divided)
1 lb Shrimp (raw, peeled and deveined)
3 Garlic (cloves, minced)
1 Lemon (juiced)
1/2 tsp Red Pepper Flakes
8 cups Green Cabbage (finely sliced)
Sea Salt & Black Pepper (to taste)
2 tbsps Sesame Seeds

Directions

1. Heat half the coconut oil in a large skillet over medium heat. Add the shrimp, minced garlic, lemon juice and red pepper flakes. Saute until shrimp is pink and cooked through (about 2 to 3 minutes). Transfer the shrimp and juices into a bowl and cover to keep warm. Set aside.

2. Place the skillet back over medium heat and add the remaining coconut oil. Add the green cabbage and season with sea salt and black pepper to taste. Saute for about 8 to 10 minutes, stirring occasionally. The cabbage is done when it is softened and starting to brown.

3. Add the shrimp and marinade back into the skillet and mix well. Divide onto plates and garnish with sesame seeds. Add extra red pepper flakes or hot sauce it you like it spicy. Enjoy!

Notes

More Carbs: Serve with brown rice or quinoa.

Leftovers: Store in an airtight container in the fridge up to 2 days.

Singing Your Own Praises

In this short video professional keynote speaker, Eileen McDargh, stresses the importance of celebrating successes every now and then to propel yourself forward with every endeavour: https://www.youtube.com/watch?v=Lcm1cMrj8ks – It gives you a sense of accomplishment as well as energy and confidence.

So if we know how to train dogs with positive rewards, to make them more effective, then why don't we use the same principles on ourselves? Why can't we look at our day and think:

"Yes, today was a great day because I did / said / achieved X, Y, Z."

We're not very good at patting ourselves on the back. On the following page is a list of 40 identified areas of education / practice / learning.

So, from this list I would like you to identify things that you have learnt, achieved, tried, watched, read, completed, passed on (to others) and / or been mindful of.

Tasks to complete:

Work Through the Table!

Have a look through the 40 identified areas of education / practice / learning and think about the areas you have really worked well through, understood and enjoyed.

It's important you look at how far you have come.

Navigating the app	Understanding macronutrients	Repeating "I'm the type of person that / who..."	Understanding hypertension
Uploading meals / photos	Identifying reasons for joining / changing	Trying a 30 day habit (adding / removing)	Understanding vegan / vegetarian needs
Asking questions	Watching the videos	Understanding obesity and its links to Covid-19	Understanding values
Completing the HEC Check	Understanding diabetes better	Understanding dietary fibre	Pinpointing why your values matter
Completing Progress Checks	Trying new recipes	Adding more fibre, daily	Understanding nutrition and the effect on chronic disease
Scheduling Weekly Chats	Understanding dietary fats better	Changing your 'story'	Understanding the difference between food and body fats
Planning meals	Identifying your healthy and unhealthy habits	Understanding osteoporosis	Trying healthy treats
Shopping better	Working weekly through new goals	Understanding nutrient cycling	Celebrating success (!)
Portion control	Understanding soreness	Trying more oily fish	Considering mindfulness
Acting on feedback	Understanding more about processed foods	Understanding sleep	Understanding hypercholesterolemia

74

DAY SEVENTY FOUR

Mindfulness and Mindful Eating

Mindfulness training (where you work out some strategies to practice, consistently) is HIGHLY effective. Science has studied large populations and looked at 'diets'. We know that this approach doesn't work without support and some of our own awareness along with techniques to manage our habits and behaviours.

Click here to watch the video:
https://www.youtube.com/watch?v=fqhYBTg73fw

Broccoli Almond Protein Salad

4 servings

20 minutes

Ingredients

- **4 cups** Broccoli (chopped into small florets)
- **2 cups** Frozen Edamame (shelled)
- **4 stalks** Green Onion (sliced)
- **1/2 cup** Almonds (chopped)
- **1/4 cup** Almond Butter
- **1 tbsp** Rice Vinegar
- **1 tbsp** Tamari (or Coconut Aminos)
- **1 tbsp** Maple Syrup
- **1 tbsp** Sesame Oil
- **1** Garlic (clove, minced)
- **2 tbsps** Water

Directions

1. In a large mixing bowl, combine the broccoli florets, edamame beans, green onions, and chopped almonds.
2. To make the salad dressing, whisk together the almond butter, rice vinegar, tamari, maple syrup, sesame oil, garlic, and water. Add more water if needed to achieve desired consistency.
3. Pour the dressing over the salad and toss to mix well. Serve immediately, or let sit for a few hours before eating. Enjoy!

Notes

Leftovers: Keeps well in the fridge up to 3 days.

DAY SEVENTY SIX

Did You Know?

The thyroid gland, which produces T3 and T4, is a small, butterfly-shaped gland in the neck, just in front of the windpipe (trachea). One of its main functions is to produce hormones that help regulate the body's metabolism (the process that turns food into energy). Both of these hormones play an important role in the regulation of your weight, energy levels, internal temperature, skin, hair, nail growth, and more.

DAY SEVENTY SEVEN

Day Off!

Book a FREE call with Gilly!

Enhance your progress with a FREE 15 minute consultation, simply see here to book:

https://p.bttr.to/2Ol0AIn

Join the community on social media:

@BetterNutritionby Gilly Facebook and Instagram

Weekly Reflection:

Think about what you have learnt this week and what resonates with you the most.

12

WELCOME TO

WEEK TWELVE

Hypercholesterolemia

Cholesterol gets some bad press. Firstly, there is a difference between cholesterol in the body and dietary cholesterol (from the food we consume). Your body makes all of the cholesterol you need and adding a small amount from foods is enough to keep you healthy. Cholesterol is a fatty substance, occurring in the body, naturally.

The Function of Cholesterol in the Body:

- It is needed to make the walls (membranes) surrounding the body's cells.
- It's the basic material that is converted to certain hormones.
- Used to absorb fat soluble vitamins.
- Assists with bile acids to help digest food.

Here is the process:

- The fat and cholesterol we consume is absorbed in the intestine.
- It is then transported to the liver.
- The liver converts fat into cholesterol.
- The liver releases cholesterol into the bloodstream.

There are three main types of cholesterol:

The Bad Guy: low-density lipoprotein (LDL):

High levels of LDL cholesterol are linked to atherosclerosis (the accumulation of cholesterol-rich fatty deposits in arteries). Unfortunately, this is what causes your arteries to narrow or become blocked. This slows or stops the flow of blood to vital organs, especially the heart and brain. Atherosclerosis affecting the heart is called coronary artery disease and may cause a heart attack. A stroke occurs when atherosclerosis blocks arteries that supply blood to the brain.

The Good Guy: high-density lipoprotein (HDL):

Higher levels of HDL cholesterol could mean you are less likely to develop cardiovascular disease (CVD). However, if a person has both a high HDL and high LDL cholesterol level they may still require treatment to lower the LDL level.

Triglycerides (blood fats):

Triglycerides are a type of fat (lipid) found in your blood. When you eat, your body converts any calories it doesn't use immediately into triglycerides. The triglycerides are stored in your fat cells. Later, hormones release triglycerides for energy between meals.

In the USA, the National Cholesterol Education Program list the risk factors for coronary artery disease as:

- Whether the person has a disease caused by atherosclerosis
- Whether the person has a disease caused by diabetes
- Being a male older than 45 or female older than 55
- Being a female with premature menopause
- Having a family history of premature coronary artery disease
- Smoking
- High blood pressure
- Not having enough good HDL cholesterol

The NHS list a further four risk factors as:

- Eating too much fatty food**
- Not exercising enough
- Being overweight
- Drinking alcohol.

**Think of trans-fats as one of the main fat contributors and consider saturated fats in moderation.

What Should My Levels Be?:

NHS Website (2020):

Check what your cholesterol levels should be

This is just a guide. The levels you should aim for might be different. Ask your doctor or nurse what your levels should be.

Result	Healthy level
Total cholesterol	5 or below
HDL (good cholesterol)	1 or above
LDL (bad cholesterol)	3 or below
Non-HDL (bad cholesterol)	4 or below
Triglycerides	2.3 or below

Symptoms:

Harvard Health (2019) report that:

> **"Most people with high cholesterol don't have any symptoms until cholesterol-related atherosclerosis causes significant narrowing of the arteries leading to their hearts or brains. The result can be heart-related chest pain (angina) or other symptoms of coronary artery disease, as well as symptoms of decreased blood supply to the brain (transient ischemic attacks or stroke).**
>
> **About 1 out of every 500 people has an inherited disorder called familial hypercholesterolemia, which can cause extremely high cholesterol levels. People with this disorder can develop nodules filled with cholesterol (xanthomas) over various tendons, especially the Achilles tendons of the lower leg. Cholesterol deposits also can occur on the eyelids, where they are called xanthelasmas."**

What to do:

The initial treatment for high cholesterol levels should be lifestyle changes. In a nutshell, a better, healthier diet and more exercise. Some people respond dramatically to dietary changes alone. Avoid processed foods (those containing trans and too many saturated fats). Instead eat more fresh fruits and vegetables, whole grains (daily) and choose your polyunsaturated and monounsaturated fats in the right portions.

Specifically, the "Mediterranean style" diet (we covered this in the module regarding disease and the 7 Countries Study). Think like the Cretens:

- Mainly eat from plant sources (fruits, vegetables, grains, beans, nuts and seeds)
- Replace fats and oils with olive oil as the principal fat for dressings and dips
- Consider some low fat, natural cheese and / or yoghurt daily (not sweetened or with additives)
- Consume oily fish 2-3 times per week
- Limit processed foods and trans-fats
- Drink alcohol in moderation
- Enjoy and respect food and meal times
- Stay active, daily

Tasks to complete:

Consider having your cholesterol tested

Have you ever had a test? Consider having a test at your local pharmacy or making an appointment to see your GP.

Use this space to record your cholesterol.

Tomato Shakshuka

2 servings
15 minutes

Ingredients

1 tbsp Extra Virgin Olive Oil
1/2 Yellow Onion (chopped)
1 Garlic (clove, minced)
1/2 tsp Cumin
1/2 tsp Paprika
1/2 tsp Sea Salt
3 cups Canned Whole Tomatoes
1 cup Basil Leaves (chopped)
2 Egg

Directions

1. Heat olive oil in a large pan over medium-high heat. Add chopped onion and cook until soft, about 2 minutes.
2. Add garlic, cumin, paprika and sea salt. Stir until combined and fragrant, about 30 seconds.
3. Add tomatoes with the juice and roughly crush with your spatula. Bring to a simmer, stirring occasionally. Stir in chopped basil. (Note: the tomato juice will reduce a bit. If you prefer a thicker sauce, leave out the tomato juice.)
4. Using a spatula or the back of a spoon, create pockets in the tomato sauce. Crack an egg into each pocket, cover the pan and cook until the eggs are set, about 5-7 minutes.
5. Scoop into separate bowls and enjoy!

Notes

More Protein: Add more eggs.
Serve it With: Toast, brown rice, or quinoa.
Make it Spicy: Garnish with red pepper flakes.
No Basil: Use spinach instead.
Extra Toppings: Top with chopped cilantro, green onions or avocado slices.

DAY EIGHTY

Recap

Reread chapters, watch those videos again or even have another go at a recipe. Use today to go back through and recap any content that you felt you needed more time on.

Tasks to complete:

Use this space to make any notes you wish.

Beef Kafta

3 servings
45 minutes

Ingredients

1 lb Extra Lean Ground Beef
1 Yellow Onion (small, very finely chopped)
1/2 cup Parsley (very finely chopped)
1 tbsp Lebanese 7 Spice Blend
1 tsp Sea Salt
9 Barbecue Skewers

Directions

1. Add all ingredients to a large mixing bowl and mix until combined.
2. Tightly pack the meat mixture into balls then form the balls into long, thin kebabs, 4 to 5 inches in length, around each of the barbecue skewers.
3. Grill over medium heat for 12 to 15 minutes, or until cooked through. Be sure to flip often so that all sides are cooked and contain grill marks. Enjoy!

Notes

Leftovers: Refrigerate in an airtight container for up to three days.
Serving Size: One serving is approximately three skewers.
More Flavor: Add fresh garlic.
Additional Toppings: Drizzle with yogurt or a tahini-based sauce.
Serve it With: Hummus, Lebanese rice, salad or on a pita.
No Beef: Use ground lamb instead.
Wooden Skewers: Be sure to soak the skewers in water prior to use.

DAY EIGHTY TWO

Reflect

We've covered a lot over the last twelve weeks, everything from macronutrients and dietary fats to sleep and healthy habits. This is your space to think about what you have learnt throughout this programme and what resonates with you the most. Think about the habits you will continue to use going forwards.

Tasks to complete:

Use this space to make notes about what you have learnt throughout this programme and what resonates with you the most.

Apple Cinnamon Porridge

1 serving

15 minutes

Ingredients

1/3 cup Oats (quick or rolled)
1 cup Unsweetened Almond Milk
1 Apple (small, peeled and finely chopped)
1 tsp Cinnamon
1 tbsp Maple Syrup
1 tbsp Almond Butter (optional)

Directions

1. Add the oats, almond milk, apple and cinnamon to a medium-sized pot. Bring to a gentle boil over medium heat and cook for 8 to 10 minutes, or until apples are tender. Stir frequently.

2. When apples are tender and porridge has thickened remove from heat and stir in maple syrup. Transfer to a bowl and top with almond butter. Enjoy!

Notes

Meal Prep: This porridge can be made ahead of time and stored in the fridge. Reheat in the microwave or on the stovetop with a splash of almond milk.

Gluten-Free: Use gluten-free certified oats if needed.

Apple: A tart apple like a Granny Smith or Macintosh works best for this recipe.

Congratulations YOU Did It!

Hey there!

We've covered quite a lot, haven't we?! How are you feeling? Better?!

This programme was designed to help you begin your journey at your own pace; it shows that with a bit of structure, care, education and guidance, you CAN stay accountable, and you CAN work towards your goals.

Maybe your motivator for starting was to lose weight, maybe it was lack of energy, maybe it was wanting to get a handle on those blasted hormones!

Often the hardest thing to do is just start, so you've already smashed that part! I hope you enjoyed it and found my information, tips and recipes useful – if you have come away even feeling a fraction more like your old self then I am super happy!

The next hardest bit is knowing what to do next. Don't worry, I've got that covered... If you would like to:

- ☐ Manage your weight so that you feel better in your clothes and look great
- ☐ Increase your energy levels so that you are ready to attack and win the day
- ☐ Reduce mood swings so that you can cope better with those curveballs
- ☐ Understand balance and food combinations to actively help you and your body
- ☐ Lose the food and exercise 'guilt' so that your life can regain its balance and fun

then my 12 week 'Happy Hormones, Healthy Weight' programme will help you get you back to the very BEST version of you that you DESERVE to be.

After all, who wants to spend the rest of their life waking up tired?!

1% Better, Daily

Gilly x

As well as my 12 week 'Happy Hormones, Healthy Weight' programme I offer a number of simple and easy monthly plans with packages to suit everyone. Services include:

- Initial 40 minutes consultation
- 6 educational post per week
- Nutrition and lifestyle analysis
- Specific goal-supported meal plan with shopping lists and recipes
- Weekly meal ideas
- Weekly meetings (30 mins)
- Access to direct messaging system
- Daily food journals with feedback
- Daily hunger-energy-cravings chart with analysis
- Weekly tasks
- 4 addition check ins per programme (for times of need)
- End consultation (40 mins)

Visit betternutritionbygilly.com/monthly-packages

email gilly@betternutritionbygilly.com

or call / WhatApp me on 07541 492 370 to see how we can work together for a **better YOU**!

Join the community on social media:

@BetterNutritionby Gilly Facebook and Instagram

Printed in Great Britain
by Amazon

69326142R00096